WRAP IT IN A BIT OF CHEESE LIKE YOU'RE TRICKING THE DOG

ISBN 978-0-9886895-5-8
Wrap It In a Bit of Cheese Like You're Tricking the Dog
A collection of new essays and emails

david@27bslash6.com

Also available by the same author:

The Internet is a Playground
Making its debut at #4 on The New York Times Best Seller list, *The Internet is a Playground* includes articles from 27bslash6 plus over 160 pages of new material.

I'll Go Home Then; It's Warm and Has Chairs
Featuring new articles from 27bslash6 along with previously unpublished material.

And Then the Robots Attacked
A collection of poetry & recipes.

The Collected Works of 27b/6 - Victorian Edition
Illustrated and abridged for polite society.

Look Evelyn, Duck Dynasty Wiper Blades, We Should Get Them
A collection of new essays.

That's Not How You Wash a Squirrel
A collection of new essays and emails.

For Seb and Holly.
Raisins.

Reviews

★★★★★ "After having 7 surgeries and arthritis in both knees, I need a shoe with a LOT of cushioning. These flip-flops provide the most comfort I have ever found in any brand. I plan on buying all the colours to wear with everything. They look great and my knees don't hurt after walking around the beach or the stores."

Shelley Smythe

★★★★☆ "If you do the math on this tub of 17, we're talking about a dollar and forty-seven cents apiece. This is expensive for dog treats but my dog loves them and she definitely makes me at least a dollar and a half's worth of happy every day."

Conor Bond

★★☆☆☆ "Decent enough first effort. The ending made no sense though. Why did Angela sacrifice herself for Jerome when they could have just jumped off the train together?"

Cheryl Edwards

★★★★★ "Super long battery life and quite bright!"
Margaret Davison

Contents

Foreforeword

"And that's when I did four lines of coke and stabbed the hooker."

"Jesus."

JM nodded, "But enough about my weekend, how's the new book coming along?" He opened his tin of Grizzly Long Cut chewing tobacco and shoved a wad in his mouth.

"Good," I replied, "a ways to go but I'm hoping to meet the deadline."

"What's this one about? There'd better not be any more bullshit about me in there. I read the last one and I never said 'Leyland Cypress grow ten feet per year', I said 'maybe a foot or two if you're lucky.'"

"That wasn't in the last book, it was in the one before with the dog on the cover. I said you kicked Amar's rubber penis under a bathroom stall door at Applebee's in the last book."

"Ah, I haven't read that one."

"Nice."

"I'm sure it's funny. It's just, you know, you do go on a bit."

"What's that supposed to mean?"

"I mean, they're not really stories, it's just you complaining about things. There's no real start, middle or end like in a proper story."

"Of course there is."

"Not like a Jack London novel."

"That's true. Perhaps I should scrap this latest book and write about the time I raised wolves to pull my toboggan across the Alaskan wilderness."

"You mean a sled, not a toboggan. Toboggans are those things kids slide down hills on. You'll need to learn the terminology if you want to write about Alaska. What's it called?"

"The book? It hasn't got a title yet. I've got a couple of names shortlisted though."

"You should call it *Shit I Made Up About JM Saying Things He Never Actually Said.*"

"You did tell me Leyland Cypress grow fast."

"Yes, but not ten feet a year."

"I'll write a retraction in the new book if it makes you feel any better. Apologise for exaggerating; that kind of thing. You're up."

JM stepped up to the stand and loaded his shotgun. He snapped it shut, bought the butt up to his shoulder and yelled, "pull!"

I pressed a button on the remote and two clays flew up and away from behind shrubbery. JM hit both and chuckled.

"Nice pair," I said, because that's something we say, and marked down two Xs on the score sheet. He had two more shots, hit both again and turned around with a grin.

"One-hundred percent, baby!"

I handed him the remote and took the stand. I hit two of the four clays.

'Hugs and kisses," JM said, marking down my score. I'm not sure if that's actual clay shooting terminology but it's something he says that means Xs and Os.

"Fifty percent."

"Yes, well, there's still a couple of stands left to catch up."

We collected our spent shells and walked along the forested path to the next stand.

"So what are the book names you've shortlisted?" JM asked.

"I'd rather not say, they wouldn't mean anything without context."

"Go on, I'll give you my honest opinion. A good name for a book can make or break it."

"That's true. Alright then, keeping in mind that these are just short-listed names and not the final."

"Yes."

"Okay, first is, *1766 Called, Your Wooden Teeth Are Due For a Scraping.*"

"That's a bit of a mouthful. What's it even mean?"

"I told you it wouldn't make sense without context."

"With or without context it's bad."

"Righto. Another on the short list is, *Wrap It In a Bit of Cheese Like You're Tricking the Dog.*

"Wrap what?"

"Again, context."

"Is the book about wooden teeth and wrapping things in cheese?"

"Some of it."

"Definitely not a Jack London novel then."

"Yes, we've established that."

"What else have you got?"

"Um, *Walter's Magic Cargo Shorts.*"

"That's the best one so far but only because it's a bit shorter than the others. You're up."

I missed all the clays.

"Skunked," said JM, shaking his head and handing me the score card. He shot seventy-five percent, blaming the one miss on me for breaking his concentration when I'd ran from a bee. I'm allergic so drop and roll is warranted.

JM spat out his tobacco, "You know what I'd call a book if I wrote one?"

"*JM's Book of Factual Things That Actually Happened Without Any Exaggerations?*"

"No, I'd call it, *The Shit I Put Up With*. Volume one of ten."

"That's not bad, perhaps I should let you name my book."

"I'd have to know what it's about first, apart from wooden teeth and cheese."

"It's shortish stories, stuff about things. I was originally going to write it just about work things and call it *Cubicle Warfare: A Guide to Office Survival* but Seb said, 'don't call it that, don't be *that* person'. I'm not sure what that means but it's just as well really as I ran out of work-related things to write about by page ten. The people I work with are not the slightest bit interesting. Yesterday, Jennifer showed me fifty photos of a Peter Pan costume she'd sewed for her cat."

"What for?"

"Exactly. That's what I said. A costume is meant to be for something. It's just sad to dress your cat up for no reason. She's not talking to me now."

"Is that going to be in the book?"

"No. Maybe. I might whack it in if I can find context."

"So, the book is about wooden teeth, cheese, cargo shorts and Peter Pan costumes for cats?"

"And other stuff. Insinkerator accidents and Christmas ties, that sort of thing. There's a bit in there about a calcified conjoined twin fetus. I thought about calling the book *Harry Potter and the Calcified Conjoined Twin Fetus* but there's probably some kind of copyright on the name. Plus, there's very little about Harry Potter in the book so it might be a bit misleading."

"Just slightly, yes."

"Holly has already vetoed the title *There's Nothing Worse Than a Confident Fat Woman. Except Transgender Old People.* She said it might be offensive to transgender old people and fat women for some reason. As if anyone cares."

"Probably for the best regardless. That's worse than the one about wooden teeth. Who's up?"

"You are."

JM shot one hundred percent, I missed all the clays and blamed the varying lengths of time between when I yelled "pull," and when he pressed the button on the remote. He told me that that wasn't it because he had an extremely consistent button pressing action and that I just needed to get my head in the game and stop overthinking it. I told him his button pressing action wasn't quite as honed as he thought and that getting my head in the game and not overthinking things cancelled each other out. JM tallied the scores.

"You need to get all four on the last stand just to make thirty percent."

"That's pretty dreadful."

"Yes it is."

"Well, hopefully we'll see some consistency in the button pressing on the last stand."

"You know what you should call your book?"

"What?"

"*Whining Like a Little Bitch: An Expert's Guide.*"

"Yes, I probably won't call it that but thank you for the suggestion. You've been very helpful."

JM chuckled, "I'm sure you'll come up with something. When's your deadline to have the whole thing finished?"

"Two weeks."

"Fuck."

"I know, right?"

"How much more do you have to write?"

"Another thirty pages or so. I asked a friend to write the foreword for me and she waffles on far more than I do so that should pad it out a bit. I'm hoping for at least twenty pages from her, anything less will be a bit of a piss-poor effort."

"Well, good luck. You're up."

I missed all four clays.

"You wouldn't survive ten minutes in Alaska," JM said.

Retraction

I would like to apologise to JM for inaccuracies and exaggerations made in my books and to correct the following quotes that are misrepresentative of what was actually said at the time:

"Leyland Cypress grow ten feet per year."
This was an exaggeration. JM's actual word's were, "Leyland Cypress grow pretty fast, maybe a foot or two per year depending on the climate and soil conditions."

"You'll need to rewire the entire thing."
At no time did JM state I needed to "rewire the entire thing" only that I should purchase an extension cable rated for exterior use rather than the ungrounded interior cable I was using to provide power to patio lights.

"I saw Amar's rubber penis drop on the floor and roll under the bathroom stall door so I kicked it back under for him."
At no time did JM say he kicked Amar's rubber penis. Amar reached under the stall door and JM only nudged it towards his outstretched hand.

"That's a big hotdog."
The hotdogs were standard size, JM just has small hands.

"And that's when I did four lines of coke and stabbed the hooker."
Again, an exaggeration. JM only stated he did two lines.

"I'm all for slavery."
At no time did JM state that he was all for slavery. He simply stated that if slavery *was* still a thing, he'd choose slaves that look like Rhianna.

"If I had to sleep with a guy, I'd probably pick Tom Cruise. He was good in the movie Days of Thunder and he's small."
JM did not state that Tom Cruise was good in the movie *Days of Thunder*.

"If the police ask, I was at your place all night. We watched 20/20 and played Trivial Pursuit. Holly won."
It wasn't the police, it was his wife Lori.

"The best part was swimming with dolphins."
JM never stated that he'd swam with dolphins, only that he'd shot one from a pontoon.

Foreword

By Patti Ford
(Insane in the Mom-Brain)

When David asked me to write this foreword I was extremely flattered. It was a touching moment, not unlike the one in *Jerry Maguire* where Tom Cruise was all, "You complete me," to Renee Zellweger. To be asked to write the opening bit of a book that tens of people would read, was an amazing honor. "My writing completes him," I thought, "He thinks I'm awesome."

Once I finished text bragging to my entire contact list (my dentist wants to know how I got his private number) and doing David Lee Roth jumps off of my sofa, I decided to bask in the glory of Mr. Thorne's adoration by re-reading his proposal. It went something like this:

Stuff about clean socks
Stuff about zombies
Stuff about a black guy and a bearded guy (2 different guys-not the same guy)
Stuff about writing another book

then:

"Write the foreword for me."

Huh.

Upon first (and obviously delusional) glance, I'd read it as a passionate plea. But upon second glance I could see that it fell just a teensy bit short of a full-on Maguire. What was I supposed to say to that half-assed request? You had me at clean socks?

So I wasn't exactly asked to write the foreword inasmuch as I was told to do so. But who cares? That's just facts, and as a person who lives in a magical world entirely made up of her own delusions, I've got no time for those. Since my superpower is the ability to totally believe whatever ridiculous thing I want to believe, I decided to decide that David flat out telling me to write this thing instead of asking me was actually a good thing. He must want me to do it pretty badly if he was too afraid of rejection to even give me the option to say no.

Then he sent me an email giving me the option to say no.

So after basking, then accidentally text-stalking my dentist, then realizing that I had nothing to bask about, then deciding that I still totally deserved to bask, then throwing caution to the wind and texting a photo of my sexiest molar to my dentist, then basking again, David sent me an email that made me un-bask. A Cameron Crowe movie this was not.

Once I decided to stop overanalyzing David's request, I realized that all of the worrying was distracting me from the fact that I had absolutely no clue how to write a foreword. So like I always do when I want to know something that I don't know (like the meaning of the term 'duck butter', which believe me, you're better off not knowing), I took to the interwebs:

How to Write a Foreword:

1) *Read the book* - According to every single editor who's ever lived, this is the number one thing you must do before attempting to write a foreword. Seeing as how your sole purpose is to introduce the book, it makes complete sense. Which is precisely why I haven't done it. This book you're holding in your hands right now? Totally haven't read it. But I'm mildly confident that it's probably okay. Most of David's books have a few good bits in them. Like that one where he found a secret skating rink, which is a lifelong dream of mine that David somehow managed to steal. Even though I hate him for living out my *Xanadu* fantasies, I must admit that I get an insane amount of joy imagining him skating around to the theme from *Chariots of Fire*. It's a vision that's gotten me through many a difficult time. Like that one time when he made me write this foreword.

2) *Refer to specific things in the book* - If you haven't actually read a book, this part can be a bit of a challenge. However, since I was born with a level of confidence that's extremely disproportionate to my level of skill, I'm willing to give it a go. This book probably has a bunch of stories about people

who annoy the crap out of David, instances where he embarrasses or injures himself in some ridiculous way, and there's absolutely no doubt that there are tangents. Oh so many tangents.

3) *Explain how you know the author* - Years ago, when David was still living in Australia, I was selling my sister's collection of American Girl dolls on eBay and he wanted to purchase one. Since he's a foreigner and English isn't his first language, I later learned that he'd failed to comprehend the exact nature of what I was selling and thought he was purchasing a mail-order American girl to be his wife. His inquiries as to which American girl would be the best choice for him should have tipped me off, but I assumed the language barrier was to blame. He also said that his turn-ons included hippophiles and Revolutionary War era clothing but as I've performed every musical number from *Annie* for an audience of my cat, who the hell am I to judge? I ended up selling him Felicity Merriman, the daring and brave 1760's tomboy. Although initially distraught to find that Felicity was not real, he became so entranced with her and her story that he ordered the remainder of my sister's collection, and every other American Girl that eBay had to offer. It was due to our transactions that he learned to speak semi-fluent English and eventually became the *Guinness World Record* holder for the most American Girl dolls owned by an Australian.

4) *Explain why the author is credible* - He's totally not. Neither am I. So good luck with all of this.

5) *Talk to the reader as if you were talking to a friend* - Are you kidding me with those pants? For the love of all that's holy, take them off, throw them in a mud puddle and drive over them a few times, pay a drunken homeless person to wear them for a week, then get them back and set fire to them. I do like the shirt, though. Is that organic cotton? It's lovely.

6) *Don't be afraid to name drop* - I've met Oprah. She told me that my shoes were cute. My shoes were not cute. They were sensible with amazing arch support, which is important since waiting in line to meet Oprah takes forever. Probably because she's so busy telling everyone blatant lies about their footwear and going on and on about how much she loves bread. I also ran into Mary Lou Retton with my grocery cart once. People that tiny shouldn't be allowed to walk amongst us normal-sized people unless they wear beanies with tall warning flags on top, or at the very least walk around making loud beeping noises or something.

7) *Mention prestigious awards* - The Nobel Prize. The Peabody. The Pulitzer. The Oscar. David hasn't won any of these. He hasn't been nominated for any of them either. I'm sure the nomination committees don't even have a clue who he is. If for some reason he ever did get an email from someone on a nomination committee, he'd just end up trolling them then publish it in a book.

8) *Explain why you are qualified to write the foreword* - I'm in no way qualified to be doing this.

9) *Remind the public of what you've accomplished* - Not a lot, actually. Had a decent poo this morning. Killed a bug that looked pretty threatening but turned out to be a wad of hair. I once ate more than half of a sheet cake before finally working up enough willpower to throw it in the trash. Fifteen minutes later I dug it out of the trash and ate the other half. There were some coffee grounds and a bit of beer on it, but that just made it taste like a crunchy, white trash version of Tiramisu.

10) *Synopsis of the book* - Here are some excerpts from emails David sent me that will give you some insight into the insight that I don't have:

September 10: The working title is *Walk It Off, Princess – A Guide to Office Survival.* If you add even one sentence about working with other people or work environments it will have enough bearing.

September 26: Ignore my email about the book title having office survival in it. And about the book being work related. It's now called *1766 Called, Your Wooden teeth Are Due For A Scraping* and it's about giant squid and robot geese.

11) *Prepare the reader for what's to come* - Who the hell knows? You could be holding a book called *Dammit, Bernice! Why Isn't The Fog Machine Fogging? I Don't Even Know How to Use A Damn Fog Machine, Henry, So Why The Fuck Are You Asking Me?* – and it might be just casserole recipes.

12) *Importance of the work you are introducing* – If enough people buy it David might finally have enough money to buy a boat. Please buy extra copies to bestow upon your enemies, because I am totally done hearing about that freaking boat. Plus, you know damn well that if he gets a boat he's gonna do something stupid on it that we will get to read about it in the next book, which will probably be titled *Everything Patti Told You Is A Lie. Except That Bit About Duck Butter. She Was Totally Right About That.*

<Edit>

David here, Patti's 'how to write a foreword' thing went on for another 38 numbers but I figured it was better to cut it short and have less pages in the book than make you slog through all of them. None of them were about how awesome I am so she missed the point entirely. Number 13 was eight paragraphs about curtains she bought and both 16 and 17 were about how much she loves the musical Annie. 28 was slightly interesting but only in comparison to 27 where she talked about repairing linoleum, 38 was an episode of Gilligans Island thinly disguised as something that happened to her, and 50 consisted entirely of the word 'Wowsers'.

Burn edge to dotted line for an exciting pirate effect.

Coloured Things

There were games in our house when I was growing up but none of them were board games. They were games my parents made me play when I said I was bored. In summer, my father would say, "Only boring people get bored, go outside and run around in the sprinkler."

In winter, it would be the bit about boring people followed with, "Why don't you blow up a balloon and tap it around the house making sure it doesn't touch the ground?"
We must have been poor because other kids had Atari. Now that I think about it, our car was pretty crap as well.

I've played board games since and am not a big fan. They take ages to set up and put away and the bit between isn't exactly a day at a water park. I used a water park as a 'fun comparison' because my partner Holly dragged me to one recently called *Wet'n'Wild* and, despite my reservations, I had fun. It was wet and relatively wild - it depends what scale you're using I suppose. If the scale ranged from 'using a different coffee mug than your favourite one' to 'bringing down a wild boar with only a knife', it wouldn't rate all that highly. Probably a sixteen. We paid extra for plastic wristbands that allowed us to skip queues and walking past others to the front of the line all day was the best part. It's probably how the Kardashians feel all of the time.

Out of all the board games I have played, Trivial Pursuit is, by far, the worst. Firstly, I don't care if the bits are called pies or cheeses, everything's a thing. Just move my thing for me and give me a coloured thing if I get the answer right. Secondly, everything else. The game takes fifteen days to play. By the thirty-eighth consecutive hour of gameplay I just want someone to win, I don't care who.

"Okay, geography, what country has kangaroos?"

"Really, David? That's the question?"

"Yes."

"Australia."

"Well done. Have a blue thing."

"I'm not on a category space, it wasn't for a cheese wedge."

"Have a blue thing anyway."

"Give me a look at the card."

"Why?"

"Just give me a look."

"Fine."

"The question was, 'The Kalinigrad Oblast borders which body of water?'"

"Mine was a bonus question."

"Right, I'm not playing if you are going to reverse cheat. It's a waste of everyone's time."

"So you forfeit?"

"No, do you forfeit?"

"Yes."

"Fine. Loser has to pack up the game. Make sure all the cards are facing the right way for next time."

There's practically nothing I wouldn't rather do than play Trivial Pursuit... that may be a bit of stretch as I'd obviously prefer to play Trivial Pursuit than spend the night in a spider cave or give a hobo a rimjob, but you get the point. I'd choose giving Holly a foot massage over playing Trivial Pursuit and I've no desire to go through all the prep, effort, mess and cleanup of moisturiser based activities unless I'm home alone. I know it's not meant to be a chore but neither is hugging after sex or remembering birthdays. Call me selfish, I can't hear you; my home office is lined with egg-cartons to block the sound of my neighbour Carl's mower.

Holly, on the other hand, grew up playing board games. The bookshelf at her parent's house is stacked with dozens of them, everything from Boggle to Trouble... I was going for an A to Z thing there but I couldn't think of any board games that start with A and the only game I could think of that started with a letter after T was Yahtzee, which isn't a board game. Neither are Boggle or Trouble really... The bookshelf at Holly's parent's house is stacked with board games, everything from checkers to Trivial Pursuit - which is Holly's favourite board game. There are other things on her parent's bookshelf of course, a knitted rooster, books about cats, photos of Holly with ex-boyfriends. I'm not the jealous type but sometimes I'll point and ask, "do you ever wonder what your life would be like if you stayed with this potato-headed zit factory with facial hair that looks like a mediaeval Scottish woman's crotch? No? I bet you do. You still love him don't you? Are you Facebook friends?"

Being Holly's favourite game, our bookshelf at home contains five copies of Trivial Pursuit, including a beat up original Genus edition, a 10th Anniversary edition, a Family edition, a *Star Wars* Collector's edition, a 20th Anniversary edition and a Welcome to America edition. They're all equally as horrid to play, even the *Star Wars* one. You'd think it would be better than the others but it isn't; nobody knows Lando Calrissian's home address or what planet produced the thread that Ben Skywalker's underpants are woven from and the type of person who might doesn't have any friends to play Trivia Pursuit with. I love Star Wars as much as the next person, don't get me wrong, I just have better things to do than learn to speak Wookiee. I wouldn't mind a stormtrooper outfit though. I'm not sure what for but it would be good to have. Even if just to wear around the house and while doing yard work. I wouldn't wear it out though, not unless it was 501st Legion certified.

The last time I played Trivial Pursuit, over Christmas with Holly's parents and her brother, I honestly thought I was going to die. On several occasions, while I waited the four hours for my next roll of the dice, my eyes rolled back in my head and I felt my body just giving up. When Holly's brother won his final thing, and the game, I almost wept with relief. As I began to pack up, Holly's father stopped me and said, "No, we play on to see who comes second."

The only thing that takes longer and is more excruciatingly tedious than Trivial Pursuit, is an office production meeting.

Production Meeting

It was Jennifer's idea to add a suggestion box to the office. She probably read about it on a HR website's *"top ten list of sad and annoying things to do in the office that give the impression you're not just shopping online all day."* Suggestion boxes are intended, I suppose, as an opportunity for employees to participate in decision making and thus feel empowered, assuming more ownership of their work environment. It showed the company cared, that feedback from staff was welcome and valued.

"Isn't that what these weekly production meetings are for?" I asked, "along with general gossip, tantrums and throwing people under a bus?"

The weekly half-hour production meeting in the boardroom was meant to ensure everyone was up-to-date and onboard with project progress and requirements. Being that our department was relatively small however, everyone had a general idea of what everyone else was working on so focus moved quickly from pretending you were on top of things - or calling out others as the cause of not being on top of things - to who didn't receive a rose on *The Bachelor* the night before, iPhone case comparison, and updates from Kevin on how well his vegetable garden is doing.

'Well, yes, in part," explained Jennifer, "but a suggestion box is anonymous. Some individuals might be hesitant to make suggestions during meetings for fear of those suggestions being belittled or thought of as stupid."

"So it's a special box just for stupid suggestions?"

"There are no stupid suggestions."

"What if someone suggests we all wear hats made out of bees? I'd need to be issued an EpiPen as I'm highly allergic."

"If you want to place a suggestion in the suggestion box about hats made of bees, that's up to you. I'd like to think that most people will add realistic suggestions that actually aim to improve workplace conditions. For the benefit of the person making the suggestion *and* others."

"Why would I suggest hats made out of bees? I was just making a point. I'm not sure how you'd even get the bees to stay in a hat shape. Plus it would be a bit annoying. Will there be prizes?"

"For what?"

"For coming up with the best suggestion. As an incentive of sorts. That way, every time someone places a suggestion in the suggestion box, it would be like entering a contest. We could give away a ham or something."

"Creating a better work environment *is* the incentive. Besides, it's anonymous, that's the point, there's no way to know who made each suggestion. Do you actually have anything constructive to add to this meeting?"

"No."

"No, I didn't think so."

A Zappos shoe box was selected as the suggestion box. A hole was cut in the lid to facilitate speedy suggestion deposit and the words 'Suggestion Box' written on the side just in case anyone forgot what it was. The creative director, Mike, complained that the boardroom table wasn't the place for an ugly Zappos shoebox so Melissa added decoupage. Cutting pictures out of magazines and sticking them on with spray adhesive gave her something to do for three or four hours and nobody dared suggest that faces of babies in the middle of sunflowers looked a lot worse than the original Zappos logo.

"That's looking good. Very colourful."

"It's not finished yet, David. I still have to apply a varnish."

"Gloss or matte?"

"Gloss."

"Nice. Where'd you find all the baby faces?"

"It's only two different babies, I made colour photocopies of them so it looks like there's more. I needed one for the middle of each sunflower."

"Yes, the babies faces in the middle of sunflowers theme wouldn't have made sense if some of the sunflowers didn't have babies faces."

"Exactly."

"You've covered up the words 'Suggestion Box' though. What's to stop someone mistaking it for sewing supplies?"

"What?"

"Cotton spools and pincushions, that kind of thing, probably buttons."

"It's got a slot in the lid. For suggestions. Why would a box of sewing supplies have a slot in the lid?"

"It wouldn't, you're right. The sewing supplies would fall out if you shook the box vigorously. I don't know what I was thinking."

"I might add the words 'Suggestion Box' though."

"Maybe you could make the letters out of tiny baby faces using the 200% reduction setting on the photocopier. From a distance, they'd appear to be normal letters but up close, you'd realise that all the letters are made up of babies faces. Or their arms."

"That's way too much work, I'll probably just cut the letters out of a magazine."

"Like on a ransom note?"

"Yes, but friendlier."

It might be assumed that such an objet d'art, set on a design agency's boardroom table between a stack of *Logo Lounge* books and a concrete pot containing plastic grass, would, at the very least, result in someone raising an eyebrow and saying, "hmm." Or men in containment suits being sent in to secure the building. People don't 'put things somewhere' in design agencies, things are placed. Things that please the eye and balance the room. There are no walnut display cabinets containing ceramic horse figurines and margarita glasses shaped like cactus. Melissa's things, however, go wherever the fuck she wants them to go. With her 'eye for design' matched by her ability to take criticism, it's best for all concerned to simply block them out.

Once, in a moment of distraction, I suggested that certain office Christmas decorations – orange and yellow streamers hung across a stairwell – were, "kind of in the way and more autumnal than Christmassy." When I went to my car that afternoon, both side mirrors were missing. I found one in a bush but it was cracked so both had to be replaced. I tried comparing fingerprints left on the mirror to prints on Melissa's monitor screen but apparently two pieces of sticky tape featuring slightly similar swirly smears isn't enough evidence for disciplinary action.

A few months back, Melissa hung a framed painting, of two ladies in Victorian attire holding umbrellas, between two advertising awards on the wall of the boardroom. It was an extreme move that screamed, 'bring it on', but nobody did. It wasn't actually that bad of a painting but then it's pretty hard to fuck up a Paint by Numbers kit. You just have to have a steady hand and clean your brushes regularly.

A month before, Jennifer signed the office up for a five kilometre staff walk to promote Alzheimer's Awareness Week. Jennifer's father suffered from it so we all feigned caring. Apparently he'd once caught a taxi to the airport and waited fourteen hours for his wife, who had died several years earlier, to come out of the women's bathroom. Which is a bit sad but at least he's not putting cats in ovens and we've all had to wait outside of airport bathrooms. I figured I'd stroll along with everyone for a bit, fall behind, and go home. I'm not capable of walking five kilometres.

I could probably manage on a bike if it was all downhill but I wouldn't because there'd be no way of getting back and I don't ride bikes because I'm not ten. Melissa was assigned the task of organizing team t-shirts featuring the company name and logo for us to wear on the day. Apparently the website was confusing or something because she ordered coffee mugs.

I made a point of taking and walking with mine, holding it up as if to say 'cheers' each time Melissa looked my way but that got old surprisingly quickly and the mug was annoying to carry so I left it in someone's letter box. I'd like to think the person who checked their mail that day was delighted to find a free yellow mug with *Your Company Logo Here* emblazoned across it. It was a pretty big mug so perhaps they use it to eat soup out of.

"Margaret, have you seen my big yellow mug? The one I got in the mail?"
"It's in the dishwasher."
"Oh no, I was going to have some soup."
"We have soup bowls."
"Yes, but I didn't want a whole bowl of soup, just a big mug."
"What about the stoneware pottery mugs? They're pretty big."
"No, they're too gritty. I'll just go without."

I realise ordering big yellow mugs instead of t-shirts doesn't have anything to do with 'artistic touches' but it does show a lack of attention to detail. Possibly flagrant disregard. I don't know how it's even possible to accidentally order coffee mugs instead of t-shirts. Melissa said she had several windows open in her browser but why was one of them for big yellow mugs? Our corporate colour is a dusty green. I had a look at the website and it's not possible to order twelve t-shirts of various sizes with one click, you have to order the large, medium, small and Kevin's XL separately. Plus, the big yellow mugs came in packs of four which means the number 9* had to have been typed in the quantity box to total the thirty-six received. It just doesn't make any sense.

"David, the client was expecting their stationery by this morning. Did you place an order with the printer for their four-thousand letterheads, two-hundred business cards, one-thousand with-comps slips and six-hundred gusset folders?"
"Yes."
"Well, apparently they've just received eighteen tractor tires. Really big ones. Do you have any explanation for this?"
"I had several windows open in my browser."
"No problem, I'll let them know."

---

* I originally had the number 11 here after asking my partner Holly what 36 divided by 4 was but then I remembered she's terrible at math and I checked on a calculator. I once cut 4 inches from the legs of our dining table based on Holly's calculations which turned out to be 3.6 inches out. When we sat at the table to test it, our knees were higher than the top. I ended up taking 3.6 inches from the chairs to fix the issue but it's like dining at a dwarf's house so we eat in bed now.

Mike tapped a folder in front of him with his Montblanc and looked around the boardroom table, "Does anyone have anything to discuss before we go over projects?"

Most of the design department was present for the weekly meeting. Jodie and Rebecca, apparently best friends now after a falling out the week before over a Facebook post about sandals, stopped comparing iWatch straps and looked around. Ben, sitting between Melissa and Jennifer instead of his usual place beside me, shook his head without looking up from his phone. Sitting in a different spot sent a strong message, a message that declared, "That's right, this is what happens if you describe copy I've written for toaster packaging as 'a bit wordy', I sit way over here. How ya like them apples?" Kevin sat in Ben's usual place. His brown polyester pants, pleats puffed out as if hiding a pumpkin, made swishing noises every time he moved. Walter, the youngest and newest member of the team, raised a hand.

"You don't have to raise your hand, Walter, what is it?"
"How long do you think this meeting will go for because I have a doctor's appointment at ten."
"Again? What did you even come in for?"
"To tell you I've got a doctor's appointment."
"Couldn't you have just rang and told Melissa?"
"I don't have any credit on my phone."
Mike sighed and took off his reading glasses, "Melissa, can you see about getting Walter a company phone? Who the fuck has a prepaid phone nowadays?"

Walter pumped a fist, "Awesome! Can I have the iPhone Plus?"

"No you fucking can't," replied Mike. He turned to Melissa, "Get him the smallest phone they have. He's not having a bigger phone than me."

Melissa made a note in her diary. The company issued everyone diaries, they were black leather bound with an embossed logo. She'd decorated hers with puff-paint. Walter sat back in his chair, arms crossed, looking dejected.

"And get me an iPhone Plus," Mike added, "Does anyone else have anything they'd like to bring up? Yes, Jodie?"

"There's ants in the kitchen area again," Jodie stated, glancing in my direction, "People should wipe down the counter if they spill sugar."

I'm not sure what happens but sometimes when I'm adding a teaspoon of sugar to my coffee, my hand does a little wiggle twitch and I miss the mug. It's not often that it happens, just when I'm least expecting it, but as I drink around twenty cups of coffee per day, not often is more often than you'd expect and when it does happen, I figure there's a chance it might happen again so there's really not much point cleaning up until then.

"How many ants?" I asked.
"I don't know," Jodie answered, "I didn't count them."
"A rough estimate will do."
"Three or four."
"So probably one."

"No, there were at least two."

"So three or four was a *very* rough estimate?"

"There shouldn't be *any* ants in the kitchen. Clean up your mess when you make one."

"Yes," piped in Rebecca, "I agree. It's common courtesy to other people who use the kitchen."

Most of Rebecca's conversations begin with, "Jodie and I both think..." and Jodie's with, "I've spoken to Rebecca about it and she agrees..." It's a symbiotic relationship that converts bitching into supported facts.

"Okay, fine," I conceded, "Sometimes when I add sugar to my coffee, my hand does a little wiggle twitch thing and I miss the cup. I'll clean it up in future. Doe's anyone else get that? The wiggle twitch thing?"

"Like Michael J. Fox?" asked Walter.

I frowned, "No, not like Michael J. Fox. He has full-blown Parkinsons."

"That probably started with a wiggle twitch thing," Walter suggested.

"It's not Parkinsons, Walter."

"How do you know? Have you been tested for it?"

"Yes, I went to a doctor and said, 'Sometimes I miss my coffee mug with a spoon of sugar so I'd like to be placed in one of those big magnet machines and be tested for Parkinson's please.'"

"MRI."

"Sorry?"

"Magnetic Resonance Imaging."

"Yes, one of those. I had to wear a gown. While I was in it, lighting struck the building and the MRI exploded. Now I can hear colours."

"That never happened."

"Can we get back to the meeting, please?" requested Mike, "I've got a busy day ahead of me so if nobody else... are we boring you, Ben?"

Ben looked up from his phone, "No, I'm listening. There's ants in the kitchen because David has Parkinson's. I'm capable of doing two things at once."

"Really? How's the Clairol copy coming along?"

"Good."

"Good as in 'finished?'"

"I'm working on it."

"It's a fucking shampoo bottle. How many different ways can there possibly be to say it makes your hair smell like coconut and Tiaré flower?"

"It's not *quite* that simple. I have to research Polynesian island culture."

"Yes, of course you do."

"Which is what I'm doing on my phone. If this was Ogilvy, they'd fly me there."

"Right, well I highly doubt that but why don't you fuck off to Ogilvy and ask them for a ticket?"

"Maybe I will."

"Good. Can you at least turn off key clicks? It sounds like someone sending morse code."

"Fine."

"Where are we on the artwork, David?"

39

While redirecting blame is a common practice in most companies, agencies have it down to a fine art. Throwing others under a bus is a skill-set listed on every designer's resumé - along with 'complaining about changes (advanced level)', 'that's not how I would have done it (advanced level 5)', and 'if they'd listened to me, it would have been heaps better (advanced level 18, gold medalist)'.

"Waiting on copy," I told Mike.

"Jesus Christ. I've got a meeting with Clairol on Tuesday, what am I meant to tell them?"

"That you're really excited at how it's progressing and can't wait to see their reaction?"

"Yes, probably, how are we doing on the Breville packaging?"

"Waiting on copy."

"Are you kidding? Do we need to fly you to Toaster Island, Ben?"

"I sent him copy," Ben replied sullenly, "It's not my fault he sent it back for changes."

"Oh, that was the toaster box copy?" I asked, "my mistake, Mister Dickens, I assumed it was your latest manuscript. I'll have Walter whack it on as it is. We can either use 2pt type or put the product photo on an inside flap."

"It was less than four paragraphs."

"It's a toaster. The product description calls for dot points, not plot twists."

"Dot points are a refuge for the illiterate."

"And a dot point in time saves nine. Anyone can change quotes to suit, Ben. Nobody's settling into a comfy chair by the window on a rainy afternoon with a hot mug of cocoa and Oprah's toaster box of the month."

"Maybe they should."

"Alright Ben," Mike sighed, "cut it down to four or five dot points and have it to David by this afternoon."

"Fine, but it means putting the Clairol copy on hold. Or perhaps you'd like that as dot points as well?"

I nodded, "That works."

Ben twitched, "I wouldn't have to put up with this at Ogilvy."

Ben wouldn't survive ten minutes at Ogilvy. None of us would. They probably record hours and expect completed timesheets containing more than coffee stains and scribbles to get your pen working.

A few years back, a coworker named Simon convinced me to play paintball. It was for his nephew's birthday and they needed to make up the numbers required for a team. I met Simon at the venue and he introduced me to his teenage nephew, four of the nephew's gaming friends, and his girlfriend Cathy - a short chubby gothic with only one hand. I'd seen a photo of her and Simon but they'd had their arms around each other so the stump wasn't evident. I learned later she'd lost the hand as a child in an Insinkerator accident which is pretty much the worst way I can image losing a hand... actually, I thought about it and came up with several worse ways but most involved spider eggs hatching so I thought it best not to list them here. Cathy still had a nub, and a smaller nub on that which was half a thumb, but it wasn't much use due to tendon and nerve damage. To be honest, it would have been a lot less creepy if she'd just lost the whole thing and worn a rubber hand or something. I shook the nub when I met her without shuddering, which I feel was pretty mature and accepting of me. It was squishy like a sausage. She was wearing some kind of purple velvet dress that ended just above her knees, striped black & white knee-high stockings, and cherry Doc's with four-inch soles. I thought there might be a bit of running around that day so I'd dressed in cargo shorts, t-shirt and sneakers. Simon was wearing a red Adidas track suit, purchased a decade earlier during a hip-hop phase, while the teens all wore skinny jeans and *Call of Duty* t-shirts - apart from one in a Minecraft singlet who mustn't have got the memo. After signing waivers and being instructed on how to use the masks and paintball guns, the eight of us were sent into a room with benches to wait for the other team to arrive. We probably should have used that time to discuss strategy but I doubt it would have made a difference. There was a game still in progress when the other team arrived. They entered and waited with us, sitting across the room on facing benches. All eight were dressed head to toe in full military combat gear. Insignia on their shoulders showed a howling wolf silhouetted against a burning moon. They owned their own paintball guns.

"So you guys have played this before?" I asked.
One of them nodded and whispered something to the others.

"We're pretty much fucked, aren't we?" I added.

They all nodded silently.

"Probably should have worn more padding..."

An orange light lit up above the doorway and our teams were ushered into holding areas at opposite ends of a large warehouse. There was scaffolding, barricades and graffitied car bodies between us. A buzzer sounded, the lights dimmed, and the holding area door opened. With no game plan, we ran for cover behind barricades and waited. It was very quiet. I could hear myself and others breathing heavily. Had the other team even entered yet? I leant towards Simon to ask and saw his head snap violently back, engulfed in green splatter from at least five paintballs striking his mask. He landed on his back, threw his gun away and crawled quickly towards the exit. Another two or three paintballs hit him in the legs and back on his way out. I heard shots and several muffled thuds nearby - the teens sprinted towards the exit a few seconds later without their weapons. Cathy, crouched a yard from me behind the same barricade, looked over at me and raised her sausage claw as if to ask, "What do we do?"

"Cover me," I yelled, hoping she would think I had a plan other than making it to the exit without being hit. Credit where credit's due; she nodded, let out a guttural scream and stood up firing. A paintball immediately hit her in the neck, just under her mask, another ten or so struck her mask and chest. She went down with a thud, flailing and screaming and firing blindly. I took at least five of her shots to my torso, two to my legs and one to my groin. The paintballs hurt a lot more than I thought they would, I'd expected a thud of sorts, maybe a light slap. It felt like being struck with a hammer and I screamed for her to stop. Another round hit me directly in the right nipple. I fired back. She was a large target and I hit her ten, twenty, thirty times. I must have advanced at some point because by the time I ran out of paintballs, I had a knee on her chest. The lights came up and Simon ran towards us. He pushed me off Cathy and lifted her mask. She was sobbing hysterically, eyes wide and mouth open. There was a fair amount of spittle and a snot bubble made it to the size of a golf ball before popping.

"Did we win?" I asked.

Apparently Simon had to take Cathy to the hospital that evening as swelling from thirty or so point-blank shots to the neck caused breathing difficulties. They broke up a few months later after she slept with a white water rafting instructor while on vacation. Simon eventually gassed himself in his car.

"You wouldn't survive ten minutes at Ogilvy," I commented, "it would be like a chihuahua joining a wolf pack. They'd tear you apart the second you started yapping."

"The fuck do you know?" Ben spat, "I'd be the pack leader."

"There's no way your tiny legs would keep up on hunts. The others would have to carry you. In a little basket or something."

"Why would I have tiny legs? I'm one the wolves, not the chihuahua."

"I'd like to be a dolphin," Melissa contributed.

"Alright," Mike interjected, "Ben, get the copy done; David, shut the fuck up. You're not exactly the world's greatest employee either."

"Exactly," Ben sneered, then frowned.

"Anyone else have anything to add?" continued Mike, glancing at his watch.

"You know what would be much better than being a dolphin?" Kevin asked, "Being a killer whale. They eat dolphins."

"Anyone else?" asked Mike.

"Well," declared Jennifer excitedly, "I *was* going to wait until the end of the meeting... but..." She held her hands out towards the suggestion box like a 1950's television advertisement model, "let's have a look, shall we?"

Sometimes during production meetings, I like to imagine what it would be like if we were all marooned on a tropical island and had to survive. There'd probably be a lengthy discussion about a rock shaped like a frog on the first day, fire and shelter mentioned as future actionable items. We'd go to sleep cold and hungry but confident we had a strategy to move forward with. On the third or fourth day, we'd eat Melissa and that night, I'd stab everyone with a pointy stick while they were sleeping just in case I was next.

Shaking the box a little, perhaps to make sure the suggestions didn't come out in alphabetical order, Jennifer opened the lid.

There were eleven pieces of folder paper inside, which was a little disappointing as eight of them were mine. As if drawing an entry in a county fair raffle, Jennifer chose one at random and unfolded it.

"Okay, and the winner is, hahaha... *'There should be an inquiry into how it's possible to accidentally order 36 big yellow mugs instead of 12 t-shirts. It just doesn't make any sens...'* David, we've spoken about this, you need to let it go."

I was mildly annoyed that one of mine had been first despite the mathematical likelihood, "You said the suggestions would be anonymous."

Melissa slapped the table, "As if anyone else would write that, nobody else gives a fuck! It was three months ago."

"Okay," Jennifer interrupted, "let's move on."

She dug into the box and selected another suggestion, "Okay then... this is another one about mugs. David, how many of these did you write?"

Melissa slapped the table again, "What does it say?" she demanded.

"It doesn't matter," Jennifer replied, "we'll just ignore all suggestions made by David."

"That's hardly fair," I objected, "I may have included valid suggestions along with those regarding mugs."

"Did you?"

"That's not the point."

"We'll go on to the next one then... okay, this is just a receipt from a parking lot."

"Yes," Kevin said, "That's mine, I had to park there for a

client meeting so I should be reimbursed. Eight dollars for one hour is highway robbery."

"That's fine, but it's not really what the box is for… let's try another one… no, not that one…"

"Is it another one about me?" asked Melissa, glaring in my direction. Her lips looked like a Muppet's crease.

"Not this one either," continued Jennifer, "…ah, here's one… *'We should be allowed to use at our desks, not everyone likes the radio to have a radio on in the design department. It doesn't have to loud.'*"

"Ha! That's mine," Walter declared.

Walter once sent me an email, marked urgent, containing the words, 'Have you got because onions?'

It was a Friday afternoon and he'd left by the time I read it and replied with, 'Have I got *what* because onions?'

The question bothered me for the entire weekend. On Monday, I received the response, 'never mind tactics' and a few seconds after that, 'tictacs.'

"What does it even mean?" asked Mike.

"Headphones," explained Walter, "it was supposed to say, 'use headphones'. We should be allowed to use headphones at our desks."

Mike stared, "Well why didn't you write that? If we'd read the suggestion after you'd left for your doctor's appointment, none of us would have had a fucking clue what it was about. It's like a whole bunch of random words thrown together."

"But can I use headphones?"

"No you can't use headphones. This isn't the local skate park or a jogging path. If I need to speak to you about something, I'm not going to wave my arms about like an idiot to get your attention."

"I have excellent peripheral vision."

"I don't give a fuck if you have X-ray vision, you're not wearing headphones. Next."

"Can I go then?" asked Walter.

"What?"

"To my doctor's appointment."

"Oh, yes, fuck off then. What's it even for?"

"You're technically not allowed to ask that," Jennifer advised, "certainly not in a group setting."

"I don't give a fuck," Mike frowned, "it's like the tenth time he's had a doctor's appointment this month. Is he dying or something? Should we start advertising for a replacement designer?"

Walter rose and swung his bag over his shoulder, "It's just a rash."

"It might be Parkinson's," I suggested.

"Or shingles," added Kevin, "if you've ever had the measles then the shingles virus is already inside of you. I saw that on a TV commercial. The guy had a shingle on his face and it was painful to wear glasses. A black lady asked him how he was doing and he said, 'don't ask.' Have you ever had the measles?"

Walter frowned, "No."

"Well it's not shingles then. Probably just a rash."

There are a lot of commercials for pharmaceutical drugs on American television. Watching an episode of *Jeopardy* will subject you to at least twenty different advertisements featuring old people finally able to push their grandkids on a swing thanks to Ethdytrin or Apibatipopyol. There's so many drug brands that the marketing teams have given up bothering to come up with clever names and adopted the Scrabble bag shake, dump, and run with it approach.

"What's this drug do?"

"It stops dry eyes by reprogramming the part of the brain that controls the tear ducts."

"Any side effects?"

"Some people reported depression, loss of vision, paralysis and death, but we'll mention that soothingly in the commercial."

"Good. What are we going to call it?"

"Well, we were thinking Fsdfwjffdghrte. Keith came up with it when he had a stroke while typing. He's on medication that thins nose hairs."

"That works. And what's this one do?"

"The Olphystraxylzen? It's a once a month injection to reduce sun glare by two-percent. It's ready to take to market, we're just waiting on copy."

"Where is it?" Mike asked, 'the rash."

Jennifer quickly interrupted, "Mike..."

"Is it contagious?"

"Mike..."

Mike raised his hands, "Fine. But now we're all just going to assume it's on his penis. And contagious."

"It's only been two appointments," Walter declared as he exited, "and it's not on my penis, it's on my inner thigh. From riding." He closed the door behind him.

"Who goes to the doctor for a rash?" asked Mike, "Twice? Put some ointment on it. What's the doctor going to tell him? 'Yes, it's still a rash, have you been riding your bike again?' Perhaps stop riding your fucking bike. Buy a car you hippy fuck."

Walter denounces motor vehicles as a socially irresponsible form of transport. Unless he has to go somewhere that is too far to ride. Other people's motor vehicles are fine then. He won't offer to pay for petrol though because that supports companies who make dolphins sew sneakers for less than minimum wage. Walter's bicycle is made by Cannondale and he calls it 'the Cannondale' instead of 'my bike'. Apparently it's a decent brand but I'm not a bicycle rider so I don't care. If I'm on my way to work and see Walter riding, I drive past really close and sound my horn. Usually it just makes him wobble a bit but he fell off once.

"I own a bike," mentioned Kevin casually.
"You do?" asked Mike, genuinely surprised, "I wouldn't have pegged you as a bike rider."

Kevin isn't known for activity and complains of chest pains if he has to park his car at the furthest spot from the entrance. People generally avoid asking him to help with anything as it means enduring a ten minute production of moaning and groaning as he gets up from his chair. Even just answering his phone is like a Shakespearean tragedy performed in sighs. He's surprisingly active in an emergency though; once when Rebecca brought in tiramisu and announced there was only one piece left in the kitchen, he pushed Jodie into a potted plant to get out the door first. It was a plastic plant so it was fine. We just had to bend some of the fronds back in to place.

"Oh, I don't ride it," replied Kevin, "But I've definitely got one in the shed somewhere. I think it needs a new chain."
"They still make chains for Penny Farthings?" I asked.
"It's not a Penny Farthing," Kevin sneered, "It's a Schwinn. They make good bikes."

Schwinn do make good bikes. In particular, the 1981 Schwinn Stingray. Featuring red and yellow trim with banana seat and butterfly handlebars, it was marketed as *'that's not my bike, it's my Stingray'* so obviously targeted at Walter's demographic. I had a chinese knock-off of the Stingray, called the Stingerbike, when I was seven or eight. I tried convincing kids at school that the Stingerbike was a much better brand than the Stingray but nobody was buying it. The fake plastic gear shifter on the frame popped off when I did a bunnyhop and one of the kids brought a K-Mart flyer to school the next day showing it listed for $34.99, well short of my $500 claim.

"Schwinn do make good bikes," Mike agreed, "I had a Stingray when I was a kid. A red and yellow one."

"Very nice," I nodded, "I had the Stingerbike."

"Never heard of it."

"Similar to the Stingray. A bit better."

Jennifer shook the box, "Okay, next suggestion..."

She read it to herself, glanced at me, and screwed it up.

"Let's try another..."

Melissa threw her arms out in exasperation, "Oh my god! The website was confusing okay? It's not my fault they have a stupid website that doesn't make sense."

"Okay, but you had to type the number 9 in the yellow mug quantity box. Where'd you get the 9 from?"

"I take a size 9 in boots."

"What?"

"It's where the Zappos box came from. Fuck, you're stupid."

I saw a movie once, I can't recall its name, about an autistic child who cracks a code he finds in a puzzle book. I think his best friend was Bruce Willis but I might be getting mixed up with the movie about the child who can see ghosts. The puzzle book code turns out to be a telephone number, which the autistic child dials, and the guys who answer are really pissed at him for working out their puzzle. I think there was a chase scene on a train and maybe a fight with a shark but I might be mixing that up with one of the Jason Bourne movies. Regardless, the puzzle guys could have saved themselves a lot of fucking about by having Melissa write their code.

"How many more suggestions are there?" asked Mike.

Jennifer shuffled the contents of the box, "Four... and a button for some reason. Let's try this one... *People should have to clean up in the kitchen if they make a mess. Otherwise we get ants.'* Okay, we've already covered that so let's go to the next one... it's just a post-it note with a drawing of cat."

"This has been a massive waste of time," Mike stated, "Was that you David?"

"The suggestions are meant to be anonymous, Mike."

"A drawing of a cat isn't a suggestion."

"It could be," I offered, "is there a question mark after the drawing of the cat? As in, 'cat?'"

"There is actually," replied Jennifer.

"Well, there you go. Cat?"

Jennifer screwed up the post-it note and selected another suggestion from the box, "Two left, let's get through these quickly shall we? Okay... *Plastic plants shouldn't be in we should have we have lots of natural sunlight in the office.'*"

"Is that another one from Walter?" asked Mike, "Is he dyslexic? What's he suggesting? That we replace the artificial plants in the office with real ones?"

Jennifer re-read the suggestion, "I think so."

"Well that's just stupid, do you know how much those artificial plants cost?"

"There are no stupid suggestions, Mike."

"Bullshit. David proved that isn't true the moment he added a question mark to a drawing of a cat and put it in the box. Every suggestion in the box has been stupid. I say we take the hideous fucking thing outside and burn it."

There were cricket noises and a tumbleweed rolled across the boardroom. A prairie dog popped his head out of a hole, popped it back in again. A few of us glanced in Melissa's direction, other's avoided doing so. Ben's head stayed down but I could see his eyes darting left and right.

"Well, come on," continued Mike. He'd crossed the point of no return so plodded on, "baby heads on flowers? What the fuck? This is a branding agency, not Grandma Clementine's crappy arts and crafts store."

Melissa put down her pen and closed her diary. It was a deliberately slow action with at least double the impact closing her diary quickly with a soft thud would have had.

"Yes, well, some people like a bit of colour, " she declared, "and babies. I know I'm not a professional graphic designer but not everything has to be black Helvaletica on a white background."

"Around here it does," Mike asserted, reaching across the table to grab the box, "a client asked what this was yesterday and I told him it was a school project the cleaner's five-year-old child left behind... did you say *Helvaletica*?"

"Alright Mike," Jennifer interjected.

"It's okay," Melissa said, forcing a smile and waving a hand dismissively, "that's just his opinion."

"Yes," agreed Mike, "It *is* my opinion. An opinion supported by twenty years in the industry, nine awards, and the words 'Creative Director' on my office door. You're the secretary."

"Chief First Impression Officer."

Melissa was pleased with her latest title. Adding 'Chief' to the front of 'First Impression Officer' gave it weight and more accurately reflected her position within the company. It had the words officer *and* chief in it now and both of those words meant something. 'Chief Executive First Impression Officer' was the next step but she'd give it a few weeks.

"Please, it's the same thing. David, back me up here, is this not the ugliest fucking box you've ever seen?"

"Art *is* subjective."

"You fucking pussy."

"Mike…"

"No, I'm going to add my own suggestion to the baby head box," Mike stated. He waved an imaginary pen in the air, "Melissa is not to design anything in this office every again, regardless of how fucking talented she imagines herself to be. And who the fuck said she could hang a painting of women holding umbrellas in the boardroom?"

He pretended to fold a giant piece of paper and place it in the box.

Mike tended to over-emphasise actions. He'd paid for acting lessons once after someone told him he'd be great in commercials. He only went to one lesson but learnt how to project digging with a giant shovel and mixing a giant cake to a stage audience. According to Mike, the acting coach said he was naturally gifted and had asked him to play the lead in an upcoming production of *Oklahoma*. He had to decline unfortunately, as it would have meant a lot of time off work.

Melissa pushed her chair back with a screech and stormed out, slamming the boardroom door behind her. She stormed back in a moment later, took the painting down, and left again without a word. We heard the front door slam and watched from the window as she crossed the parking lot and tossed the painting into a dumpster. It would have been more dramatic had it been a better throw as the painting bounced off the lip and she had to pick it up toss it in again. On her way back, she glared and held her middle finger up towards the window.

"It's reflective glass," commented Mike, "She can't see in. What makes her think we're even paying any attention to her?"

The reflective glass in the boardroom is a constant source of entertainment. People regularly check their hair and clothing as they pass by. Sometimes people lean against the window and they jump when you bang on the glass. Once, a homeless man took a dump. Mike chased him off with a poster tube and Melissa had to wash the turds down a drain with a hose. The water pressure is pretty low at work so it took her about an hour. There was a bit of carrying on and a lot of dry-retching so we closed the blinds.

"You owe her an apology," said Jennifer.
"The fuck I do," replied Mike, "someone had to say it. And thanks for your support, David. I'll remember that."
"Why do I have to follow you down the rabbit hole?"

"Because you started the whole thing with your stupid suggestions. Oh look, there's one left in box, let's have a read, shall we?"

"That's probably not necessary."

"No, I insist. Let's see... *'I suggest we never adopt hats made out of bees as the office uniform. It would be dangerous.'* Yes, I agree. Excellent suggestion. Hands up of all those in favour of never adopting hats made out of bees as the office uniform. Very fucking helpful, David."

I thought there'd be more suggestions from others. Boring suggestions about thermostat regulation or printing on both sides of paper to save ink. As it was Jennifer's idea, you'd think she'd have contributed at least one tedious suggestion herself. It's like holding a party and telling everyone to bring a dish but not bothering to make anything yourself. Then commenting that their dip isn't that great and they should try adding more paprika next time. Maybe use a nicer bowl. It had been a fairly successful production meeting though; I never saw the suggestion box again so at least something came out of it.

We wrapped it up after another brief discussion about ants, a lengthier discussion about puff-paint not sticking well to leather and leaving bits everywhere, and an estimate from Kevin on how many bags of Sphagnum Peat Moss he thought he'd need to buy for a 10'x30' garden plot. Nobody was in much of a rush to leave the boardroom because it meant walking past Melissa's desk.

We played rock, paper, scissors, finger to see who went first. It's similar to the standard game but every now and then you throw in the finger as your play. It gets a few chuckles and someone says, "Yes, okay, come on, just play it properly."

"You alright, Melissa?" I asked as I headed towards the stairs.

"Yes, of course I am," replied Melissa, "Why wouldn't I be? I'm just the secretary."

"Right. Oh, Jennifer asked me to give this to you." I put the parking lot receipt on top of her monitor.

"Mm hm."

"I was just joking about the mugs."

"Mm hm."

"And I actually thought the painting wasn't bad. Good balance of light and dark. It reminded me of a Bob Ross."

"I've no idea who that is," she replied, "because I'm just the secretary."

"That's going to get old pretty quick."

"It was actually a paint-by-numbers kit."

"Really? You'd never have guessed."

"I know, right?"

I watched Melissa climb up onto the dumpster and fish the painting out just before closing time. My office overlooks the car park and I spend much of my afternoons flicking rubber-bands onto the roof of Ben's car. My record is 274 rubber bands and 18 pens but that was on the one day he parked almost directly under my window. She dusted the painting off and put it on the backseat of her Ford Fiesta before driving off.

5 Ways To Lose a Hand That Would Be Worse Than an Insinkerator Accident

1. Cutting your hand while camping, perhaps on a can of beans, and that night while you are sleeping, a spider crawls into the cut and lays eggs. A week or so later - I don't know how long spider eggs take to hatch - baby spiders eat your hand from the inside out.

2. The same as #1 but with wasps instead of spiders.

3. Insinkerator-based hand loss but instead of the Insinkerator being turned on, it's flicked off and on. I'm assuming this would be worse as it's slower but I'm not sure. Maybe you'd appreciate the breaks. I probably should have thought about this one a bit more but it was originally also about things hatching and I changed it at the last minute.

4. Putting your arm between elevator doors to stop them closing but they don't register and trap you there. Then someone inside the elevator skins your hand with a potato peeler. This one's a bit of a stretch, I probably should have called this page '2 ways' instead of 5.

5. I don't know, putting your hand in a toaster and turning it to the crumpet setting?

David's Bin

I heard Jodie fart this morning. I actually heard her fart three times - four if you count the little squeak at the end as she made a final check.

She hadn't seen me when she walked upstairs and sat at her desk - I was under mine plugging in my laptop cable. I popped my head up when I heard the first fart, it was like one of those fake ones you make by licking your arm and giving it a raspberry, one with a lot of spit. Her back was to me and I watched as she lifted her left cheek and farted again. The first must have been a test run because the second ran for triple the time and at a much lower pitch. It was like a drawn out sigh mixed with the sound of a flag flapping in a strong breeze. The third was shorter, softer, and faded out like a librarian saying 'shhhhh'. The fourth, as mentioned, was just a small squeak - or like that water-drop noise some people can make by flicking their cheek.

At the sound of someone walking up the stairs, Jodie quickly wafted the air behind her with a hand. Mike stepped off the landing and made a face.
"Jesus fucking Christ, what's that smell?" he asked.
"I know," Jodie replied, nodding and making a distasteful face, "I smelled it when I came up. I think it's David's bin."

Raymond

I watched a boy named Raymond kill a nest of baby birds when I was eleven. He was older than me, by three or four years, the brother of a boy in my class. I don't remember that classmate's name or why I'd ridden with him to his house after school but I remember Raymond calling us into the backyard. There were four baby birds in the nest, eyes barely open but strong enough to raise their beaks and make a ruckus. Perhaps they thought they were about to be fed. An adult bird, a sparrow I think, hopped from branch to branch above us making angry noises. Raymond held the nest in one hand and smiled. He held a tennis racquet in his other hand.

Afterwards, as I was riding my bike home, I began to cry. Not because of what *he'd* done, but because I hadn't tried to stop him. Because I'd stood there watching him throw the nest into the air and swing at it, watched him pick up a baby bird he'd missed and throw that into the air and swing again. I cried because when he'd laughed, I'd feared the repercussion of doing or saying anything that showed disapproval, and I laughed as well. I stopped my bike, put my head on my handlebars and sobbed, replaying my laugh over and over in my mind. There was a rock, slightly larger than my fist, laying by the side of the road. I picked it up and turned my bike around.

Raymond answered the door when I knocked. There was only a few feet between us and I threw the rock as hard as I could. There was a lot of anger in my throw, at him and myself. Blood splattered my face and the door as he went backwards onto the floor. For a moment he was still and I thought he was dead, then he gurgled, spat blood onto his cheeks, and groaned. I turned, picked up my bike, and rode home.

I was in bed when the police arrived. It must have taken them some time to get my information from the school registry. My mother was away with my sister at the time, chaperoning a school trip; my father answered the door and invited them in. He knew why they were there as I'd arrived home splattered in blood. I put a dressing gown on over my pyjamas and sat on the edge of the bed, waiting for the police to walk down the hall, open my door, and take me to jail.

Later, my father said that he had told the officers how Raymond had killed the baby birds and that I had tried to stop him and had been threatened with the tennis racquet. The damage to Raymond's face hadn't been as bad as it looked, a busted nose and lip. The police put it down to boys being boys and chose not to file charges. I should have been pleased about that I suppose, relieved at least, but it hadn't been boys being boys, it was the day I realised how weak and fearful I was, how I'd conformed, given approval to cruelty to protect myself. My father's lie was who I should have been, not who I was.

I was riding home from school a few weeks later when I heard a shout behind me. Looking back, I saw Raymond and three other boys around his age riding their bikes after me. Perhaps I should have ridden faster, attempted to escape, but instead, I stopped. They broke my bike, one of the boys kicked it over and jumped on the spokes. I was kicked from behind and went down, kicked again in the shoulder, my collarbone snapped. I heard ringing, a kick to an ear, to my testicles, to my teeth. The beating was severe, but quick. It was less than a few minutes before Raymond and the boys got back on their bikes and rode off.

There was a bus stop shelter no more than thirty feet away and from it, an old man, perhaps in his sixties, had watched the beating in silence. He walked over, held out a hand.
"Are you okay?" he asked.
I winced as he helped me up.
"I would have done something but... I thought..."
I nodded.

Perhaps he'd chided himself afterwards, played out preferred scenarios in his head. Or maybe a lifetime of self-preservation had made it the norm, the obvious and only choice. I wheeled my bike home and told my parents I had lost control on a steep hill. I had to wear a sling and eat puréed bananas for a few months but my collarbone mended and my front teeth were replaced. I wasn't able to ride while my arm was healing and I was on a bus the last time I ever saw Raymond.

It was a couple of months after the beating and I was on my way to school. The bus pulled up at a stop for someone to alight and from my window at the back, I saw Raymond on the sidewalk below. He was sitting on his bike, a foot or so from the curb and several feet ahead of me, smoking a cigarette and talking to a girl. He was facing away and hadn't noticed me. I waited until the door sighed closed and the engine revved before opening my window. As Raymond passed below, I reached out and grabbed his hair.

A nicer ending to this story might have been if I'd encountered a group of bullies picking on a small child or throwing rocks at a kitten, and, putting my own safety aside, chose to stand up to injustice. Or perhaps rescuing Raymond himself from bullies, or quicksand, and becoming friends in the end. That's not how things work though and kids are assholes.

I managed to hold on for almost two blocks before I lost my grip. The bus was doing perhaps forty or forty-five miles per hour at that stage and I watched out the back window as Raymond rolled and bounced along the road. He covered a fair distance. I closed the window and smiled.

Tiny Houses

I saw a show on television tonight called *Tiny House Hunters.* It was about poor people who have decided to decrease the square footage of their living area from two or three thousand square feet to under two-hundred by moving to live in a camper trailer. None of them said, "I'm poor and I'm going to live a trailer" of course, they justified their decision by claiming environmental responsibility, or the desire not to be part of the mortgage rat-race, or a love of being able to hitch up their house and travel wherever they want. None of them travelled anywhere though, they parked their 'tiny house' on their parent's property, which their parents must be fucking delighted about.

"You've bought a house? I'm proud of you. I was wondering when you were going to make your way out into the world on your own. You're forty-five after all."
"Yes, as of this morning, I'm officially a home owner. It's a lot of responsibility but I'm ready to take it on."
"Well, if you need any help moving your stuff let me know."
"That won't be necessary, there isn't room for any of my stuff in the new house so I'm going to leave it all here."
"What if you need something?"
"I'll walk across and get it. I'm parking my house in the backyard. Do we have any spare extension cables?"

Free Book!

Mowing the Mishler Way!

Packed with mowing tips by mowing expert Carl Mishler

Learn how to:
- Mow
- Blow Leaves
- Make paths to your neighbors'
- Mow

Mowing the Mishler Way!
by Carl Mishler

"The best day to mow is every day!"

Simply fill in your details below and mail this page or a copy to:

Carl Mishler Mowing Expert
PO Box 144
New Market, VA 22844

or fax to: 540-740-8354

Yes! Please send me my free copy of Mowing the Mishler Way!

Name: _____

Postal address: _____

_____

An Excerpt From
Mowing the Mishler Way!
by Carl Mishler

Hello, my name is Carl and I love mowing. I'm sure you love mowing as well otherwise you probably wouldn't be reading this book. We should hang out sometime. Between 6.30pm and 7pm works best for me as I like to catch the *Wheel* and *Jeopardy* before bed time. We can sit outside and look at my lawn if it's not too cold. Maybe bring a light jacket just in case. And a chair.

People often ask me, "Carl, what's the best time of the day to mow the lawn?" which is a silly question as most ride-on lawnmowers these days have headlights. I like to start mowing around four in the morning, have a little break for lunch, then mow until six-thirty each evening. Sometimes I'll skip lunch or have a sandwich on the mower though.

When I'm mowing, I like to pretend that I'm riding a horse. Before I put my mower in gear, I say, "Hi ho, Silver away!" and chuckle to myself. My wife Toni thinks it's hilarious. I could probably be a professional comedian if I had the time but the mowing isn't going to do itself. Maybe in the future but hopefully I'll be dead well before that happens. The Jews invented robots.

One of the many benefits to mowing all day is the social interaction with neighbors. I've cut a path to all their yards and I carry a tape measure with me at all times so I can check their tree branches aren't overhanging the borderline. I own a gun and I'm not afraid to protect my property.

When I'm mowing my lawn, I like to wave to the neighbors as they drive past. Sometimes they'll stop their car and say, "Hello Carl, your lawn's looking great," and I reply, "Thank you, the trick is to cut it on the second highest setting and fertilize twice a year. What are you doing tonight between six-thirty and seven?" I don't wave to the Negros that live at number 308 though, I've seen them drive past slowly, checking out my brass hose fittings. I know what's up and I know who complained about my confederate flag and the bonfire I had last week. This is America, I'll burn a cross in my front yard if I want to. Go back to the Sahara and spear tigers if you don't like it. Same goes for the Muslims and Mexicans. When Trump is president, he's going to sort out this mess. He's a business man.

I once killed a man with a crossbow.

10 Emails From Walter
That Make No Sense

From: Walter Bowers
Date: Thursday 10 September 2015 10.13am
To: David Thorne
Subject: No Subject

Bugs in your office. not bugs stinky beetles?

From: Walter Bowers
Date: Monday 28 September 2015 2.07pm
To: David Thorne
Subject: No Subject

Are you sweet i am. someone needs to batteries the air conditioner before we all suffocate. AAA. 2 of them.

From: Walter Bowers
Date: Wednesday 14 October 2015 9.26am
To: David Thorne
Subject: No Subject

Hear the engine in the water cooler?

From: Walter Bowers
Date: Monday 9 November 2015 3.11pm
To: David Thorne
Subject: No Subject

I forgot it was today. Can you they have m&ms and comfortable seats. You don't have to wait in the car. they have good magazines too. I might not go though. i'll let you know before 4

<hr>

From: Walter Bowers
Date: Friday 20 November 2015 1.20pm
To: David Thorne
Subject: No Subject

Do I nod like its ok to Jodie if she says please instead of just telling people to do? Its just manners bitch.

<hr>

From: Walter Bowers
Date: Thursday 3 December 2015 4.45pm
To: David Thorne
Subject: No Subject

19 12 64 2 14 3 18 6

From: Walter Bowers
Date: Monday 18 January 2016 9.22am
To: David Thorne
Subject: No Subject

From: Walter Bowers
Date: Wednesday 17 February 2016 11.43am
To: David Thorne
Subject: No Subject

That's what happens wet it gets wet then you get rust. Its easier to oil it before it gets clean the rust off. Not my problem anyway.

From: Walter Bowers
Date: Tuesday 8 March 2016 12.16pm
To: David Thorne
Subject: No Subject

This works because of angles.

....

From: Walter Bowers
Date: Wednesday 18 May 2016 4.01pm
To: David Thorne
Subject: No Subject

Nobody the spiral machine. We should someone should show us how. I don't know do you? I can make the holes but the spiral in it. i hate it.

....

From: Walter Bowers
Date: Monday 6 June 2016 9.50am
To: David Thorne
Subject: No Subject

That wasn't beyonce.

UGHHH

I quite liked Laura the first time I met her. First impressions are never that reliable though. I once met a guy named Neil Fairhead who I got on well enough with over beers to accept an invitation to his house for dinner the next night. When I arrived, he was dressed in a skin-tone latex body suit with breasts. There was a plastic painter's drop cloth on the living room floor and a video camera set up on a tripod. He did make a pretty decent gnocchi though.

I first met Laura at my friend JM's house a few years back. She was dating JM's son Joseph, living together actually, and seemed unpretentious if a bit quirky - admirable personality traits. She was short and round and dressed as a banana. It was Halloween and there were thirty or so guests in outfits ranging from 'piss poor' to 'well, at least you tried'.

Holly and I had put some effort into our costumes as Holly takes it all pretty seriously. She starts planning what she is going to be for Halloween the day after Halloween as it takes 364 days to perfect her outfit. That year, she'd decided to dress as Neytiri from the movie *Avatar*, and had to start getting into her costume two days before the party as it involved prosthetics, airbrushing, and an animatronic tail. As Holly likes us to have couple's costumes, I went as a tree.

"Are you a piece of broccoli?" Laura had asked.

"What? No, I'm a tree. Are you a lemon?"

"No, I'm a banana."

"Why?"

"I like bananas. They're rich in fibre and an excellent source of vitamin B6."

"Righto."

"Why are you a tree?"

"Good point. Someone always gets the rough end of couple's costumes. Is that Joseph over there in the gorilla outfit?"

"No, I've got no idea who that is, Joseph is dressed as a lumberjack from the future."

Joseph was wearing a plaid flannel shirt and had taped a glow-stick to the blade of a hatchet. It was definitely at the piss-poor end of the scale. I get on well with Joseph even though he's a Redditor and has a beard. I'm fairly accepting of all types. Except gays, blacks, Jews, buskers, deaf people and Morgan Donnelly who co-anchors the local WHSV news. She looks like a creepy Victorian era vampire doll. I paid a lot of money for my television and shouldn't have to put up with that shit. The guy who does the weather isn't much better, not Greg, he's okay, I'm talking about Justin. Aubrey's nice enough, she just needs to lose a few pounds.

Joseph and I were Facebook friends and a week or so after the Halloween party, Laura sent me a friend request. I'm not a huge fan of Facebook as it mostly consists of people posting photos of things they did when I wasn't there. If I wasn't there, I don't give a fuck. If it seems like something I might have enjoyed being there for, fuck you for not inviting me. A photo of your cat? Didn't need to be there and the cat looks like every other cat on the planet. A photo of you drinking beer around a fire pit with a dozen or so other people I know? I hope someone throws a bag of gunpowder and nails in.

I accept most friend requests but I delete them the second they post religious quotes, more than two photos of a cat in a row, stuff about mistreated dogs that need a home, photos of their car, photos of their haircut, photos of them mountain-bike riding or playing frisbee golf, and anything to do with 'movember', astrological forecasts or fun runs. I only have four Facebook friends left and even those are on thin ice. One of them, my Albanian friend Raf, posted a video of himself listening to music in his car yesterday. It was some Arabic sounding women wailing about something miserable while people smashed crockery and slaughtered a goat in the background.

Laura's posts were innocuous enough. There was the occasional cat photo but most were recipes or life-hacks. That sort of thing. They rarely made double digit Likes though most received one or two, usually from her mother and Joseph. She posted a photo of a pumpkin she had carved and I clicked Like. Out of pity really, it looked like a child with cerebral palsy had just bashed at it a bit with a spoon then called it a day.

The next time I saw Laura was at a polo match. I know you're probably thinking, "Oh, a polo match, well tally ho and pip-pip my good fellow," but it wasn't like that. One of my four Facebook friends, Murdock, is Facebook friends with the son of a family who owns the winery that hosts the polo matches. He'd invited a group of us up for their opening day and Holly will go to a gate opening if there's wine. A week before the polo match, Laura had posted a selfie on Facebook. She was wearing a scarf around her head, and shucking corn for some reason. I'd commented something about fulfilling her quota for the Soviet motherland and to watch out for bears. It was a throwaway comment but Laura embraced it. It was something interesting. About her. As such, she decided to change the word 'the' to 'ze' in all her sentences. It reflected the new interesting Laura, the one who looked Russian.

"Ze horses must get tired running up and down ze field all afternoon."
"Sorry?"
"Ze horses. Zay must get tired."
"Yes, maybe. They're horses though, probably used to a bit of running about. What's with the 'ze' instead of 'the'?"
"What ze instead of ze?"
"You keep saying 'ze' instead of 'the'. It's pretty annoying."
"Do I? I hadn't noticed."
"Really? I would have thought it would take quite a bit of concious effort. Maybe it's a weird form of Tourette's."
"Hmm, maybe."

Laura researched Tourette's online that night. It was something else interesting. About her. She looked Russian *and* might have Tourette's. It was *two* winning tickets in the interesting lottery. The next time I saw her, at a friend's karaoke party, she'd adopted and perfected a series of involuntary movements and vocalizations, mostly shudders and grunts.

"I love zis song. It eez one of my UGHHH favourites."
"Jesus, what the fuck was that?"
'Sorry, I haz ze UGHHH Tourette's. I grunt."
"Since when?"
"Last week."
"Are you sure about that? Tourette's usually shows up during early childhood. It's not something you catch."
"UGHHH"
"Oh, you're up. Rhythm Of The Night by Corona."
"Zis eez ze rhythm of ze night, ze night, UGHHHH oh yeah, zis is ze rhythm of ze UGHHH night."

People were paying attention. Facebook posts detailing her daily battle with Tourette's garnered more comments and Likes than she had ever received for photos of herself shucking corn. She added epilepsy and Lyme's disease to her list of ailments. The Likes multiplied and comments made it to the length where they required a 'read more' link. She added whooping cough, Asperger's syndrome and altitude sickness. I bumped into her at the supermarket a month or so later.

"You're in a wheelchair?"

"Yes, UGHHH zis allows me access to ze day to day things most people take for granted."

"Where'd you get it?"

"I set up a GoFundMe UGHHH account."

"Seriously? How much did it cost?"

"Thirty-five UGHHH hundred dollars. It's custom fitted."

"You don't think you're pushing this whole thing a bit?"

"What zing?"

"All of the 'zings'. What's the oxygen mask for?"

"Chronic obstructive UGHHH pulmonary disease."

"Right. And the leg braces?"

"Rickets."

"Really? Should I ask about the bell?"

"Leprosy."

A few weekends back, JM invited Holly and I to go camping on a forested property he owns called Deer Camp. Each year around this time, he goes up to clear the trails and cut firewood in preparation for hunting season. It's nice up there at this time of the year, the autumnal* leaves and light jacket weather are a dramatic contrast to the bitterly cold wasteland it becomes during December and January.

---

* *The word autumn comes from the Latin word autumnus, meaning 'passing of the year'. After the Roman era, the word continued to be used as the Old French word automne and by the 16th century, autumn was in common use in English. Americans prefer the word 'fall' because it's when leaves fall down. This simplification also accounts for the words blinkers instead of indicators, flip-flops instead of thongs, weed whacker instead of grass-trimmer and feet-clothes instead of socks.*

JM's son Joseph went up that weekend as well and Laura joined him. It had been a while since she had been able to get out, what with the Spina Bifada and testicular cancer. Joseph had traded in his car for a van - with a motorised ramp system for Laura's chair - and pulled up around four in the afternoon. He would have been there earlier but Laura had discovered a lump on her neck that morning that turned out to be a calcified conjoined twin fetus. She named it Kal-El because she'd always wanted a brother. With a lot of whirring and clanking and a series of beeps, Joseph lowered Laura to the ground and pushed her chair towards the fire-pit, locking a wheel so she couldn't roll away and wrapping a shawl around her shoulders. Due to her alopecia, he also popped a beanie on her bald head.

"You're looking well," I said. It wasn't true but as the saying goes, if you can't say anything nice, something something two in the bush.

"Zank you, UGHHH," Laura replied from behind dark sunglasses, she was now legally blind.

"Can I get you a beer?"

"No zank you, I haz to learn to do zese UGHHH zings myself." She reached shakily towards an open cooler with her Nifty Nabber™ extension claw; arthritis had left her hands gnarled.

"Tell me UGHHH when I'm getting close."

"I would, but that would be enabling. Just how long are you planning to keep up this bullshit, Laura?"

".. Laura?"

"Sorry, I fell asleep. I have narcolepsy. What did I miss?"

"I was asking how long you think you can keep up this charade."

"Whoops, zhere I go again. How long was I out?"

I haven't seen Laura since the camping trip. Which is a pity as she's a pleasure to have around. Due to having the bends and lycanthropia, she only leaves her decompression chamber to howl at the moon. I get regular Facebook updates though, usually thirty or more per day. Today, she posted that she had rigamortis, Lou Gehrig's disease and Alzheimers. A few minutes later, she posted the same thing. It showed attention to detail so I clicked Like.

Answering Ben's Emails For Him While He's Out For The Afternoon

From: Margaret Harper
Date: Thursday 9 June 2016 11.43am
To: Ben Townsend
Subject: Flyer changes

Hey,

Are you able do the Barry thing this afternoon?

Maggie

....

From: Ben Townsend
Date: Thursday 9 June 2016 12.06pm
To: Margaret Harper
Subject: Re: Flyer changes

No, but I can do saults.

From: Margaret Harper
Date: Thursday 9 June 2016 12.14pm
To: Ben Townsend
Subject: Re: Re: Flyer changes

What's saults?

Maggie

....

From: Ben Townsend
Date: Thursday 9 June 2016 12.17pm
To: Margaret Harper
Subject: Re: Re: Re: Flyer changes

Somersaults.

From: Robert Dawson
Date: Thursday 9 June 2016 12.03pm
To: Ben Townsend
Subject: Re: Business card layout

Ben, they like the layout but can you make the font a bit bigger (the target audience is retirement age) and change the border to blue?

Thank you, Rob

From: Ben Townsend
Date: Thursday 9 June 2016 12.22pm
To: Robert Dawson
Subject: Re: Re: Business card layout

Hello Rob,

I can certainly make the changes but as we are well over-budget on this project, I will have to charge $12,000 as additional.

Ben

From: Robert Dawson
Date: Thursday 9 June 2016 12.29pm
To: Ben Townsend
Subject: Re: Re: Re: Business card layout

I hope that's a typo. Why would it cost that much?

From: Ben Townsend
Date: Thursday 9 June 2016 12.32pm
To: Robert Dawson
Subject: Re: Re: Re: Re: Business card layout

I'm thinking about buying a boat.

From: Melissa Peters
Date: Thursday 9 June 2016 11.51am
To: Ben Townsend
Subject: Client briefing

Jeff rang. He said the meeting is at 3 today. Do you know where his office is?

....

From: Ben Townsend
Date: Thursday 9 June 2016 12.12pm
To: Melissa Peters
Subject: Re: Client briefing

Bitch do I look like a compass?

From: Jason Greene
Date: Thursday 9 June 2016 12.37pm
To: Ben Townsend
Subject: Meeting Thursday

Hi Ben

Do you need me to arrange a projector for tomorrow or do you have your own for the presentation?

Jason

From: Ben Townsend
Date: Thursday 9 June 2016 12.43pm
To: Jason Greene
Subject: Re: Meeting Thursday

Hello Jason,

A projector won't be necessary as I intend to present the packaging concepts through cosplay. As such, I might need to change the meeting to Friday as my mother hasn't finished sewing my costume yet.

Ben

....

From: Jason Greene
Date: Thursday 9 June 2016 12.47pm
To: Ben Townsend
Subject: Re: Re: Meeting Thursday

Are you serious?

....

From: Ben Townsend
Date: Thursday 9 June 2016 12.52pm
To: Jason Greene
Subject: Re: Re: Re: Meeting Thursday

I know right? She doesn't understand that people have deadlines to meet.

From: Kevin Eastwood
Date: Thursday 9 June 2016 12.11pm
To: Ben Townsend
Subject: Walker copy

How are we going on the Purina project? They were expecting to see revised copy today. What do you want me to tell them?

Kevin

....

From: Ben Townsend
Date: Thursday 9 June 2016 12.15pm
To: Kevin Eastwood
Subject: Re: Walker copy

Tell them the copy is exactly the same as the previous version but I've replaced every eighth word with a photo of the Hubble telescope as requested.

....

From: Kevin Eastwood
Date: Thursday 9 June 2016 12.20pm
To: Ben Townsend
Subject: Re: Re: Walker copy

Nobody requested that.

From: Lauren Townsend
Date: Thursday 9 June 2016 11.48pm
To: Ben Townsend
CC: Jamie Townsend, Sarah Townsend
Subject: Moms birthday <3

Hi, I looked at prices on the new Kindle and if we all 4 of us put in, it's $35 each. If that's ok I'll order it tonight. x
Lauren

....

From: Ben Townsend
Date: Thursday 9 June 2016 12.36pm
To: Lauren Townsend
CC: Jamie Townsend, Sarah Townsend, Janet Lynch
Subject: Re: Moms birthday <3

Bit steep for me. You guys go thirds, I'll make her a mixtape.

From: Graham Sullivan
Date: Thursday 9 June 2016 12.34pm
To: Ben Townsend
Subject: Bowling

Sorry about Saturday. I forgot I promised Vicky I'd help her move. Still friends? :)

From: Ben Townsend
Date: Thursday 9 June 2016 12.34pm
To: Graham Sullivan
Subject: Re: Bowling

I promise no matter what, I will never be your friend and I will hate you for the rest of my life.

From: Evan Manning
Date: Thursday 9 June 2016 12.12pm
To: Ben Townsend
Subject: June crossfit fun run

I'm picking up the t-shirts today. What size do you want?
Evan

....

From: Ben Townsend
Date: Thursday 9 June 2016 12.19pm
To: Evan Manning
Subject: Re: June crossfit fun run

3XL please. I like them baggy.

From: Aisha Gaddafi
Date: Thursday 9 June 2016 10.06am
To: Ben Townsend
Subject: Greetings from Aisha

Hello Dear,

Permit me to take your moment to inform you of my desire to go into relationship with you, as I have prayed, and I need a trust-worthy person in my project. I am the daughter of the Late President of Libya, Late President Muammar Gaddafi. I don't want many people to know about me because of my position and my family popularity, as such, please treat this letter very confidential. I don't want to involve any other person in this matter please. I want to trust you and you alone. Thanks.

Before my father died, part of the valuables he secured which I have the details, is Gold of great value, worth $750,000,000.00. After the death of my father, I quickly ran to Algeria. When, I got to Algeria, I was not feeling very safe and secured, so I wrote to the United Nations and they took me to Oman Muscat. I herein solicit for your kind assistance of funds for a plane ticket to fly to your country so that you may help me invest this money. I will give you 30% for your efforts. I join you in your country soon to live comfortably and invest.

Thank you and May God bless you.

Aisha Gaddafi

From: Ben Townsend
Date: Thursday 9 June 2016 12.49pm
To: Aisha Gaddafi
Subject: Re: Greetings from Aisha

Dear Aisha,

I'm very sorry to hear of your troubles and of course I will do anything to help. Please find my credit card details below. It has a high interest rate so please don't buy anything but the plane tickets and let me know when you're on your way.

Ben

BEN C TOWNSEND
VISA 4147 2022 4835 2398 Exp. 04/19
(CVV 813)

hey grl, i lik yr herr

Smiling & Nodding

"I've never been to a funeral," Walter said, "What do I wear?"

"A wetsuit is fairly standard," I answered, stirring my coffee and brushing spilt sugar from the counter with my hand, "you've never been to a funeral?"

"No... well maybe when I was a kid but I don't remember what I was wearing. Do I have to buy a suit?"

"You already have a suit. Wear the black one you wore to Mike's dinner party last week."

Mike and his partner Patrick hold dinner parties at their apartment fairly regularly. Patrick is a vegetarian so none of the food is edible but it's important to go because if you don't, everybody talks about you. "So, where's x tonight?" is code to begin a group evaluation of the absent person's personality, work ethic, hygiene, wardrobe, hairstyle, and likelihood of being the one who left a floater in the bathroom. There's an air about the office for at least a week when you miss a dinner, a circle you stepped out of. Those that attended have longer kitchen conversations, smile knowingly when they pass each other in the hallway, make each other friendship bracelets. Comments such as, "Oh that's right, you weren't there, you missed out on a really great cucumber and pine-nut risotto," really mean, "We're all best friends forever and you might be getting fired."

"That isn't a suit," Walter replied, "The jacket and pants don't match. The jacket has a herringbone texture and the pants are dark blue. That's why I sat down the whole night."

"I didn't notice and I doubt anyone at the service would care if you wore happy pants. I've seen people wear *beige* pants with a dark jacket and tie."

"I have to buy a tie?"

Walter was wearing cargo shorts and a Boba Fett t-shirt the day he arrived for his interview. He'd ridden his bicycle and was shown into the boardroom still wearing his helmet. I'd held back a chuckle and kicked Kevin under the table. We were holding the first round of interviews for Simon's replacement in Mike and Jennifer's absence. It would be a quick interview, I thought, wondering how Walter had even made the list. He was barely out of his teens and the position required an experienced designer - someone with 'an eye'. We chatted for a bit, then I asked to see his portfolio to get it over with.

"You better fucking not have," Mike had said over the phone, "you're going to have to apologise and explain that you didn't have the authority to offer him the position."

"No, he starts Monday. I offered him the position because I didn't want him going to an interview anywhere else. You'll agree with the decision when you see his portfolio."

"It's that good?"

"I took it upstairs to show Jodie and she cried."

"Actual tears?"

"A pretty solid glisten."

"Is he a cocky little shit? Does he have one of those stupid haircuts that's shaved on the sides with a bouffant on top?"

"No, it's more like a mop I think. It was hard to tell as he was wearing a bicycle helmet. And no, he's not cocky, he's a nice kid. Kevin talked to him for twenty minutes about cabbages and he took notes."

"Does he have a fat gothic girlfriend with a weird stump instead of a hand?"

"I didn't ask but it seems unlikely."

"Jennifer's going to have a fucking fit when she gets back, I get to pretend to be angry with you so she doesn't get angry with me. I'll write a stern email or something."

"That's fine."

"Have you told Simon?"

"No, I saw him this afternoon but I didn't tell him we'd held interviews this morning."

"Fuck him. You don't quit in the middle of a client meeting and then expect your job to be waiting for you."

"He said he'd rather be stabbed than ever have to design a business card or logo again anyway."

What's he going to do then?"

"Make bowls apparently."

"Make what?"

"Wooden bowls. He owns a lathe."

"No, I mean what's he going to do for money?"

"Sell bowls."

"To who?"

"People who like wooden bowls I assume. To put keys and

sunglasses in."

"He's going to starve."

Surprisingly, Simon hadn't starved. After creating a clean website and branding his product well*, one of his bowls was featured on a website called Houzz and, shortly after, on a popular HDTV kitchen makeover program. He received over 1200 pre-orders for his 20 inch $430 shallow Maple-burl bowl named *Horizon* on the first day alone. I have one on my dining table to put keys and sunglasses in.

Simon and I didn't get along very well when we worked together. We butted heads often, both of us looking for reasons to do so, and niggling regularly become shoving. He'd filed a total of sixteen formal complaints against me and we'd sat through at least five meetings with Jennifer to resolve conflicts. He once threw a screwdriver, across two rooms with a corridor between, which embedded itself into a wall a few inches above my head. I could have lost an eye which would have prevented me from ever becoming a professional tennis player. It's easy to take depth perception for granted. He'd thrown the screwdriver after discovering I'd removed all the screws from his office chair but, really,

---

* *Uppercase Gotham Demi, with a decent amount of kerning, below a circular graphic of varying line thicknesses representing tree rings for those interested. Simply describing something as 'branded well' means nothing to designers; It could be Pentagram standard or the offal someone without a single defining talent or clue throws together because they own a copy of Illustrator. Like Rian Chandler Dovis. That's right, if you're reading this Rian, your shit is dreadful.*

who gets back from lunch to discover a screwdriver and 46 screws on their desk and *still* sits down? It was meant to collapse into 16 pieces when wiggled but instead, he'd looked up at the air vent suspiciously and plonked himself down. What air vent takes 46 screws? I'd removed the screws in retaliation for him removing the exterior knob and spindle on the men's bathroom while I was in there earlier. I'd heard a rattle and yelled, "Occupied!" but hadn't guessed what was happening until I tried to leave. I had to kick the inside knob off and poke a plastic toilet brush handle into the square hole where the spindle had been to get out. Removing the bathroom knob was retaliation for hiding half a tin of tuna in the air vent in Simon's office, which was retaliation for him changing the alert tone on my computer to a K.D. Lang song, which was retaliation for changing his email signature to 'Bobby Beige, Fashion Expert', which was retaliation for him saying, "K.D. Lang rang, she want's her haircut back." I'd been feeling self-concious about my new haircut before he even made the comment.

It was as much a surprise to Simon and I as everyone else that we became friends after he left the agency. Or maybe we'd been friends the whole time. Intertwined with the childish antics and bickering, had been a mutual love of good design and a respect for the other's experience and knowledge. There was an undeclared ceasefire the moment discussion turned to a logotype's kerning, the appropriate grid for a layout, tweaks to turn a good design into award winning work. There were no niceties, no 'It's pretty good but have you thought of's', only junior designers require delicacy and praise. We ripped into flawed design like lions on a crippled antelope. It took me a couple of weeks after Simon left to stop walking into his office with proofs. The third time it happened, I emailed him to see how he was doing.

From: David Thorne
Date: Friday 6 June 2014 2.54pm
To: Simon Dempsey
Subject: Hey Princess

Hey,

Just thought I'd check you haven't killed yourself. It's pretty quiet around here without you.

David

....

From: Simon Dempsey
Date: Friday 6 June 2014 3.03pm
To: David Thorne
Subject: Re: Hey Princess

I bet it is.

From: David Thorne
Date: Friday 6 June 2014 3.09pm
To: Simon Dempsey
Subject: Re: Re: Hey Princess

It is. I put a cardboard box on your chair so that when I look across into your office and squint my eyes, it's as if you're still here.

David

....

From: Simon Dempsey
Date: Friday 6 June 2014 3.17pm
To: David Thorne
Subject: Re: Re: Re: Hey Princess

Yeah I watched a dog take a dump today and thought of you. I suppose everyone had a good laugh about me leaving.

....

From: David
Date: Friday 6 June 2014 3.28pm
To: Simon Dempsey
Subject: Re: Re: Re: Re: Hey Princess

Why are you watching dogs take dumps? And no, not really. It was a dramatic exit so some gossip is to be expected but everyone here has been through a breakup at some point in their lives. We were concerned, not amused. I thought the bit where you couldn't open the boardroom door after you quit was fairly amusing though.

David

From: Simon Dempsey
Date: Friday 6 June 2014 3.37pm
To: David Thorne
Subject: Re: Re: Re: Re: Re: Hey Princess

I know, I've opened that door a million times so I don't know why I was trying to pull it. Is Mike angry?

From: David Thorne
Date: Friday 6 June 2014 3.45pm
To: Simon Dempsey
Subject: Re: Re: Re: Re: Re: Re: Hey Princess

Mike's always angry. He wheeled his chair outside this morning and left it on the curb because a wheel squeaked. He made Melissa run out and get it ten minutes later when someone stopped their car to have a look at it.

David

From: Simon Dempsey
Date: Friday 6 June 2014 3.51pm
To: David Thorne
Subject: Re: Re: Re: Re: Re: Re: Re: Hey Princess

Lol. Hey, could do me a favor and check the second drawer down on my desk and see if there's a white Seagate hard drive there?

From: David Thorne
Date: Friday 6 June 2014 4.01pm
To: Simon Dempsey
Subject: Re: Re: Re: Re: Re: Re: Re: Re: Hey Princess

Yes there is. Is it full of porn? It's not amateur home video of you and Cathy is it? Dear god, I hope not.

David

From: Simon Dempsey
Date: Friday 6 June 2014 4.12pm
To: David Thorne
Subject: Re: Re: Re: Re: Re: Re: Re: Re: Re: Hey Princess

It's not porn dickhead. It's backups. I've got my programs and typefaces on there as well. I'll ask my dad to pick it up

sometime next week if that's ok. Can you leave it at the front
desk with Melissa?

....

From: David Thorne
Date: Friday 6 June 2014 4.18pm
To: Simon Dempsey
Subject: Re: Re: Re: Re: Re: Re: Re: Re: Re: Re: Hey Princess

I'm leaving in half an hour. I could drop it off at your place
on my way home if you'd prefer. Maybe stop and have a
coffee if you're not doing anything. I've been working on a
logo for a white water rafting company I wouldn't mind your
opinion on.

David

....

From: Simon Dempsey
Date: Friday 6 June 2014 4.23pm
To: David Thorne
Subject: Re: Re: Re: Re: Re: Re: Re: Re: Re: Re: Re: Hey Princess

Hilarious. Ok. Sounds good.

There *was* porn on the drive. I had to check. It was mostly Japanese Animé porn though, which was a bit disappointing. One of the videos was about a woman with both male and female genitalia. She had a giant crystal sword and wore a bikini space suit for some reason. There was a lot of yelling and running fast, and a flashback to when she was a famous pop-singer, then she had sex with some kind of half man, half rock-monster, who also had both genitalia, while floating in space. When they reached climax, there was a lot of flashes and a planet exploded. Back on earth, a lady holding a small boy's hand pointed up at a bright light in the night sky, presumably the exploded planet even though there's no way light travels that fast, and the boy did a little excited running on the spot dance and shouted, "Naya nomble can!" It was pretty dreadful but who am I to judge? I've closed browser windows and sat silently for a few moments thinking, 'What's wrong with me?' many times. The last time was after watching a Youtube video on how to build your own swimming pool out of railway ties.

"You don't own a tie?"
"Well, one," Walter answered, "but it has a penguin on it."
"A small embroidered penguin?"
"No, its a pretty big penguin. He's ice skating."
"Is it a Christmas tie?"
"No. Just a penguin ice skating tie."
"Well that should be fine then. If anyone asks if it plays *Jingle Bell Rock* when you squeeze it, you can say, 'no, it's not a Christmas tie, it's just penguin ice skating tie.' Is the penguin

wearing a scarf and beanie?"

"No... actually, it might be now that I think about it. It's been a while since I wore it."

"Last Christmas?"

"No, to a movie premiere."

"You wore a tie to a movie premiere?"

"I thought premiere meant you had to dress up. You know, with a red carpet and stuff. I'd never been to a premiere before."

"Was the movie *Happy Feet*?"

"No, I can't remember what it was called but it was about an Indian kid and a tiger in a boat."

"*Life of Pi.*"

"No, it didn't have any pies. Just tigers and boats."

"And an Indian kid. The movie is called *Life of Pi.*"

"No, I'm pretty sure it isn't. You must be thinking of a different movie. Can I borrow a tie?"

"Sure."

Walter was rather upset that I'd forgotten to bring him a tie so we stopped at Target on the way to the service. He made me go in with him, because it was my fault he had to, while Jennifer, Mike and Jodie waited in Jennifer's Prius. I didn't mind as it was cramped in the back seat, what with Jodie being pretty much circular. She was alway on a diet but it was that one where it's ok to eat six hotdogs and a family-size bag of chips for lunch. Really, when all days are cheat days, they're just days. Nobody's swept up in the performance so just shut the fuck up and eat the cake.

Once, during a three-hour drive to an out of town client, Jodie ate four full size Snickers and a loaf of sliced bread.

Only the five of us from the office were attending the service, I thought there would be more but the others had 'stuff to do' or 'didn't really know him very well, you know, outside of the office'. There's a difference between having worked with someone and having worked together I guess, but I still found it disappointing. Walter was going and he'd never even met Simon.

Simon's dad had called me just after 11pm. He'd used Simon's phone so I answered with, "What's up, fuckstick?"

Simon's sister Janet had been the one who found him. She'd let herself in to his apartment and heard the car running in the garage. I wasn't aware it was even still possible to asphyxiate yourself by running a pipe from the exhaust of your car to a window. I thought the catalytic converter, standard on vehicles since the mid-eighties, removed most, if not all, of the carbon monoxide. I Googled it and apparently there is still enough produced, it just takes a lot longer. Descriptions contained conflicting information on the result though; some said the occupant of the car would feel drowsy, fall asleep and die peacefully in ten to fifteen minutes, other's said it would be painful, that there would be vomiting and convulsions. I hope it was the former. I wondered what Simon had been wearing at the time; had he dressed up for the occasion or not bothered? Had he listened to the radio or sat in silence? Had he cried or just sat there with a 'come on, let's get this over with' look on his face? He didn't leave a note but he did shut down his website and refund unfilled orders that day.

I hadn't even known Simon was sad, let alone suicidal. I'd seen him the week before and he seemed fine. We drank beer and smoked cigarettes in his shed while shellacking wooden bowls. I can't remember everything we talked about that evening but I'm fairly certain the subject of running a pipe from his car's exhaust pipe hadn't come up. I do remember him laughing at a face I pulled when he explained what shellac is and when I told him about Jennifer's idea to incorporate a suggestion box at the office.

"Why aren't we wearing gloves for this," I'd asked.
"Because you wouldn't be able to feel the grain. You may as well be spraying it on if you're wearing gloves."
I held up stained hands, "What takes varnish off? My nails look like Ben's teeth."
Simon passed me a metal can and a rag, "It's not varnish, it's shellac."
"That's not just the brand name?"
"No, varnish is a polymer , shellac is a natural product and food safe. It's actually an excretion from the female lac bug."
I made a face.
"It seals better than varnish or oil, gives a deeper, richer shine. I think it's worth the extra effort. I saw Cathy last week, did I tell you?"

"No."

"At the hardware store. She was in the checkout line."

"And?"

"And nothing. She didn't see me, I was behind a DeWalt power tool display. She was buying a shelving system."

"The wooden type or those wire ones?"

"The wire ones."

"Cheap arse bitch."

"Yeah, they're alright for linen cabinets though. They let the fabric breath. She looked good."

"Really? So she's given up on the whole gothic thing, grown her hand back and lost 200 pounds?"

"Wiccan and no, but her hair's blue now. It's funny how girls move on a lot faster than guys."

"Yes, it is. I once asked Holly once how long it would be before she'd start dating again if I died and she said, 'not for at least three months'. Says a lot really. She'll probably be downloading Tinder at my funeral."

"I know, it's like they have a 'next' button... I wonder who helped Cathy put up the shelves."

"Hey, did I tell you Jennifer's decided to introduce a suggestion box at work?"

"That's a good idea. It shows feedback from employees is valued."

"Fuck I'm glad I don't work with you anymore."

Simon chuckled.

I'm not sure I've ever been truly depressed. I've been sad of course, at times so sad it was almost unbearable, but I think depression might be something different. It might be a degree of sadness I haven't yet reached, or perhaps it isn't about sadness at all. Maybe it's an absence of any feeling. Like when a coworker tells you about their weekend or shows you photos on their phone of their cat, but times ten.

Our production manager, Rebecca, sews outfits for her cat Jack. I'm not sure why. I guess she was just sitting around one day and thought, "Fuck this shit, I'm forty and single, time Jack had a Peter Pan costume."

"And here's a close up showing the detail on his felt hat."
"Right, but what's it for?"
"What do you mean?"
"Is it for a costume party or something?"
"He's Peter Pan!"
"Yes, I can see that, but why?"
"Because it's adorable!"
"Okay."
"And here's one of him sleeping."

I've seen photos of Jack dressed as a pirate, a fireman, a cowboy, a fish, and Edward Cullen without feeling anything. Not even pity for the cat. It's one of those fluffy ones with the pushed in face, the kind that stares at you with disgust as if to say, "Who invited you to Endor?" I'm not a fan of any type of cat but if I'm watching a news report about one being rescued from a burning building and it turns out to be the fluffy pushed in face kind, I'm particularly disappointed.

"What do you think?" asked Walter, holding the tie up for Jodie to admire. It was dark blue with grey triangles. Jodie nodded her approval and Walter reached into the front of the car to show Mike and Jennifer.

"Very nice," Jennifer affirmed, reversing out of the parking space, "And very fashionable. It looks just like Mike's."

"No it doesn't," Mike frowned.

"It's the same colour."

"Your Prius is the same colour as my Lexus. That doesn't make it a Lexus. We should have taken my car. There's more leg room and it makes noise. I keep thinking you've stalled at traffic lights."

"I get almost fifty miles to the gallon."

"Who gives a fuck? Are you on food stamps?"

"It was the best one there," Walter continued, "David tried to convince me to get one with stripes but this one was better. It was a bit more expensive but it was the best one."

"How expensive?" asked Mike. We'd agreed to put it on the company credit card.

"Twenty-five dollars," answered Walter, "but it was definitely the best one."

"That's not expensive for a tie," said Mike, "the one I'm wearing cost over two hundred. It's the Ermenegildo Zegna Tokyo tie."

"I like mine better," replied Walter.

"That's because you're a fucking philistine," Mike replied.

"I like Walter's better too," I said.

"Bullshit you do, you wish you owned this tie. What are you wearing? A boring black tie. Is it even silk?"

"I think so, it's Ralph Lauren."

"Oh my god, nobody wears Ralph Lauren anymore. They sell it at TJ Maxx."

I actually like TJ Maxx. They have good soaps. There's a TJ Maxx in the same plaza as the supermarket where Holly and I shop. Sometimes she suggests popping in to have a quick look and I sigh and say, "Oh, okay then," but really I'm quite pleased. While Holly browses, I head straight to the soaps and give each a good sniff. By the time Holly's done, with a trolley full of cushions, photo frames and designer dog toys, I'll usually have thirty soaps in a 'we're definitely getting these' pile and another ten or fifteen in a 'smell this, what do you think?' pile. There's a third pile but that's just a 'I don't want this but check out the packaging' stack. We have an entire cupboard full of soaps at home. Sometimes I stand in front of it and open and close the door really fast several times so I'm fanned by the combined scents.

Actually, I've only done that once or twice, I usually have much better things to do. I didn't want to leave the impression that I just stand around at home wafting the smell of soap towards myself. I spend far more time watching television and yelling at the dogs. I also read sometimes and we have a meth-lab in the basement. That Pepsi aint eight-balling itself.*

---

* *It's actually Holly's candle-making area. Don't call the police.*

"There's nothing wrong with TJ Maxx," I said, "They have good soaps. I'm using a cantaloupe & oregano one at the moment."

"Do they have Penhaligon's?" Mike asked.

"Is that a Harry Potter thing? "

"Exactly."

"It's also a good place to buy socks, you can get a six pack for five-dollars. Or do you only wear two-hundred dollar socks?"

"They're Mario Bresciani. Signature collection."

Walter was pleased with his tie and that's all that mattered. He tied and retied it several times on the way to Simon's service, perfecting the knot and length and looking down to admire it often. I glanced over at him and he gave the tie a little flap at me. I smiled and nodded, he smiled and nodded back proudly. It was like the end of a movie about two cops, one a stickler for the rules and the other a shoot from the hip renegade, who become friends after blowing things up but nothing needs to be said because a smile and nod says more than words ever could. Then their captain calls them into his office and lists all the damage they did and you think he's angry but then he also smiles and nods and says, "Good job, guys." The two cops glance at each other, confused, and one asks, "So you're not taking away our badges?" and the captain replies, "not this time." That kind of opens it up for a sequel in which a politician demands they do lose their badges - for doing something reckless at the start of the movie that saved the life of a young child but was public enough that they had to be made an example of - but they chase the bad guys anyway and this time they blow up bigger things, including a plane. In doing so though, they save the politician's family and at the end of the movie, the politician smiles and nods as he places bravery medals around their necks at a ceremony. The two cops smile and nod at each other and their boss smiles and nods from the audience, maybe gives a thumbs up even though his arm is in a sling from being shot. I gave Walter a thumb's up, which was supposed to be the end of the exchange but he gave me a thumb's up in return then pointed at the back of Mike's chair and quietly mouthed the word, "Jealous."

Jodie, sitting between us and taking up far more than a third of the back seat, shook her head.

"What did you write in your speech?" she asked.

"It's not a speech," I replied, "Simon's dad just asked me if I'd say a few words."

"Okay, but what did you write?"

"I didn't write anything. I'm just going to wing it."

"Oh my god."

I'd never met Simon's father but he was exactly how I'd pictured him; a short balding man wearing a grey cardigan with wooden buttons over a white shirt and tie. He approached us as we stood as a group awkwardly inside the entrance and introduced himself as Keith. We gave our condolences, Jennifer gave him a hug which was nice, then we all stood around in a circle nodding for a bit before Keith headed off to mingle. Simon's sister Janet waved from across a crowd of twenty or so people and made her way over. I'd met her a few times when she'd visited Simon's place to help pack bowls into boxes and print shipping labels but we hadn't talked much. She worked as a caregiver, whatever that means, for a retirement home that was on the news a few years back for reportedly mistreating old people. I can't recall exactly what the accusations were but it had something to do with residents being washed with towels soaked in petrol to get rid of bed sores or something. It turned out to be only one resident, and methylated spirts not petrol, but he did have to go to the hospital with minor burns. I remember watching a news report at the time; the reporter approached a group of Cribbage players at a table and a wrinkled old lady looked up, clasped her hands together, and asked, "Are you here to save us?" I mean, come on, it's not Hollywood Edith, no need to ham it up. Suck on another Werther's and move your plastic pegs, everyone's had enough of your nonsense.

"Interesting choice of photo."
"Sorry?"
I nodded towards an easel displaying a large image of Simon smiling. He must have been 15 or 16 when the photo was taken and was wearing a McDonald's uniform.
"Was it his first day at work?"
"I like that photo," said Janet defensively, "what's wrong with it?"
"I'm not saying there's anything wrong it, just that it's an interesting choice. It's like an employee of the month picture, or a 'before' photo from a Proactiv advertisement."

"Okay."

"You couldn't find a more recent one?"

"No, not one where he looked so happy."

"Oh, right. Can't argue with that. Probably best not have a photo of him looking sad because... you know..."

"Yes."

"The suicide."

"Yes, I knew what you were referring to."

"I feel bad for mentioning it now. The photo I mean... and the suicide."

"It's fine.

"So how have you been?"

"It's been a difficult week."

"Yes, I'm sure it has. I meant generally though."

I'm not great at small talk. Apparently the key is to ask questions and show genuine interest in the answers but who has genuine interest on tap? Even if I manage to keep it up for a couple of rounds, eventually the facade cracks and we stand around nodding until someone says, "Well, I might go grab one of those toothpicks with a piece of cheese and an olive stuck on it before they're all gone."

Mike nudged me, "Check out the tragedy near the iced tea table," he whispered, "it's like Addam's Family cosplay."
She was all in black with a brimless 50's hat and black lace veil. Her velvet dress stopped just above the knees showing fishnet stockings and 12-hole Doc Martins. Her back was towards us but I knew who it was instantly.

The first time I'd met Cathy was at a paintball game. There was a bit of contact back forth after that in regards to medical expenses but she'd signed a waiver so didn't have a case. The second time I met her was at one of Mike and Patrick's dinner parties. She was only there for about five minutes and Simon was banned from ever inviting her again; you don't visit someone's house for the first time and throw a bowl of spinach & artichoke dip across a room, even if someone does ask you if you're just stopping by on your way to an *Insane Clown Posse* concert. We were both civil the third time we met, other people were in the line at Subway so I just gave her my order and watched her make my 12" sub closely in case she tried to give me old lettuce.

The fourth and final time we met was at Simon's house, Cathy turned up while we were hanging a Rothco print above his fireplace and wanted to talk to him. I left. They tried getting back together but it only lasted a week. Simon couldn't put her 'accident' with a white water rafting instructor behind him and Cathy hadn't exactly kept herself chaste since. He'd checked her phone while she was taking a shower and discovered several messages containing photos of her vagina sent to a fellow sandwich artist. Apparently they were taken in the Subway bathroom so I hope the hand washing procedures are enforced.

"Jesus Christ, that's Cathy" I sighed, "What the fuck is she doing here?"

The attendees, mostly elderly, had left a clearing of several feet around her. Possibly to avoid being singed should she suddenly conjure Satan. If I hadn't known Cathy, I might have felt sorry for her. Probably not though. She turned, recognised our group, and headed towards us. I turned away quickly.

"Goddamit. Pretend we're in the middle of an important discussion."
"About what?"
"Yes, I agree, traditional Haida art certainly does display many of the components found in modern logo and corporate identity design..."

Cathy touched me on the shoulder, I turned giving what I hoped was a 'slightly annoyed at being interrupted' look.
"Oh, hello Cathy."
She pantomimed a sad face and held out her arms as if expecting me to rush into them.
"Sorry, I don't do hugs. I have a thing."
"About hugs?"
"No, just a thing. What can I do for you?"
"I just wanted to say hello."
"Hello." I turned back to Mike, "So, as I was saying, you have to connect the green wire to the copper ground otherwise it might give you a shock."
"There's no need to be rude," Cathy stated at a volume above the general level of the room, "I'm grieving too you know."
A few people looked our way.

"Yes," I replied, "you certainly look the part. Were they having a hat sale at Widows'r'us?"

"No, asshole," Cathy puffed out her veil, "I bought it on Amazon. What's your problem?"

"Apart from the level of your voice right now?"

Cathy looked around, noticed the stares. She lowered her voice and leant in, "I knew Simon a lot longer than you did, I've got just as much right to be here as you."

"Nobody said otherwise, I'm just surprised you bothered."

"Why wouldn't I? I cared about Simon very deeply."

"Not as deeply as you took that white water rafting instructor's co..."

"Is there a problem?" Simon's father asked, approaching with his brow furled.

Jennifer stepped in, placed a hand lightly on his back, "There's no problem at all, Keith. Emotions just running a little high, you understand. David and Simon became close friends over the last six months and he's just a little protective and emot..."

"We were a lot closer," Cathy interrupted.

Jennifer pursed her lips, "It's not a competition, Cathy, I'm sure you and Simon shared a very special connec..."

"We were fireflies."

"...Sorry?"

"It's from my poem. For the service."

"Dear lord," I said.

Jennifer pinched my arm, I flinched.

"Mike," Jennifer said, "weren't you and David about to head outside for a quick cigarette before the service begins?"

"No," Mike replied.

Jennifer glared.

"Fine," Mike said, pushing me towards the door, "We'll be right back. In the meantime," he pointed to Cathy, "don't let Jizzo the Clown anywhere near the dip bowls."

I'm not a huge fan of poetry. I'll accept the argument that it's an art form - being an expression of the imagination - but by that broad definition, so are Etch A Sketch drawings and Magic Aqua Sand sculptures. I don't think anyone *really* likes poetry, apart from the ones writing it, and they only *really* like their own. People declare they like poetry but if pressed to name their favourite poem it's generally a struggle;

"Oh, um, probably *The Road Less Travelled*. It's a classic."

"The 1978 book of psychology and spirituality by M. Scott Peck?"

"No, the poem version. I had to read it in school. It's about a guy who's taking a walk and chooses an overgrown path. It's a metaphor for not worrying about ticks."

"Do you mean *The Road Not Taken*?"

"No, that's a movie about a dad and his son who have to escape from cannibals after the apocalypse. I think Liam Neeson was in it."

I sat at the end of our row, with Walter, Jennifer, Mike and Jodie to my right, so I wouldn't have to shuffle past knees when it was my turn to say a few words. We'd been asked to make our way into the room where the service was being held by a man wearing a blue suit and were seated three rows from the front. Cathy sat in the front row defiantly, dabbing her eyes with a handkerchief because that's what they do in the movies. Simon's coffin, closed, was on a raised pedestal behind a podium. It was honey pine which Simon wouldn't have been pleased about. Walter leaned over, pointed and whispered, "Is he in there?"

"No," I replied, "That's a truck driver named Larry."

"Alright. Just asking. I didn't know if they put him in there afterwards. To make it lighter to carry around."

"It lowers after the eulogy and is cremated. They don't pause to carry the body in and plonk him in."

"It's weird that he's in there though."

"Yes it is."

The man in the blue suit took the podium and thanked us for coming before speaking of Simon's life - a life "short but very bright." He spoke of Simon's childhood, his collection of hand painted Lord of the Rings figurines, his talent for 'pottery' and the lives he'd touched. It was standard fare but professional. Empty but delivered with warmth.

"And now," the man in the blue suit said, "one of Simon's close friends is going to say a few words...."

As I began to rise out of my seat, Cathy leaped up and whispered something to the man.

"Oh, apparently this young lady..."

"Cathy."

"Cathy has written a poem she'd like to share first."

He stepped aside from the podium, Cathy took his place. She cleared her throat and unfolded a piece of paper.

"Fireflies," Cathy said, pausing for a dramatic eye dab.
"I was searching, calling.
You called back, mirroring my pitch and luminosity.
I bobbed and flickered towards you.
You bobbed and flickered towards me.
We met halfway on a branch and embraced.
Who knows how long fireflies live?
A night? An eternity? Does it matter?
For a night or an eternity, our lights were twice as bright."

Cathy folded the piece of paper and gave the pantomime sad face again. Waiting, I suppose, for applause. Perhaps a standing ovation. She added a little nod.

"Okay, thank you," said the man in the blue suit, taking the podium again and indicating for Cathy to take her seat. She dabbed and nodded. Halfway back to her seat, she turned and returned to the podium, bending the microphone towards her, "I printed out extra copies of the poem if any of you would like one to take home. Just come and see me afterwards. They're free."

The man in the blue suit waited until Cathy was sitting before continuing this time, "And now one of Simon's friends is going to say a few words. David?"

I waited for a moment to see if Cathy would leap up again, then made my way to the podium.

"Okay, firstly, my condolences to Simon's family. For his loss and that poem. I Googled 'how long do fireflies live' on my phone while Cathy bobbed and flickered back and forth from the podium and apparently it's two months if anyone was wondering."

Cathy glared at me; I heard Mike chuckle.

"Secondly, Simon enjoyed woodwork, bowl turning to be specific, not pottery. He and I spent many late nights in his shed fulfilling the hundreds of orders he received for his bowls. I wasn't allowed to use the lathe but I became quite good at shellacking. The trick is to rub it into the grain with your fingertips even though it would be a lot easier to spray it on. His attention to detail, even the smallest of details, was infuriating at times, but it what was made Simon *Simon*. It was why he was so good at whatever task he undertook, be it a two-hundred page annual report with Venn Diagrams or turning a simple wooden bowl. He cared. I once asked him why he bothered doing a fourth coat of shellack on the bottom of bowls when it would never be seen and he replied, 'If a job's worth doing, it's worth doing well.' Which was a bit annoying as I'd quoted that years earlier to him regarding items super-glued to his desk and he'd just stolen it. I shellacked the bottom of bowls a fourth time while we drank Amstel Light and argued about design and music and pizza toppings. He was happy when he was working in his shed. Happier than he had ever been working as a graphic designer at our agency. In a way, he had Cathy here to thank for that, if she hadn't slept with a white water rafting instructor while on holiday with her sister, it's unlikely he would have quit."

Several people whispered to each other. Cathy sunk low in her seat, her double chin doubled and her face scowled.

"Thankfully, he got over the breakup fairly quickly. It was only a matter of days before he met Emily, a model, and they began dating. She was intelligent, beautiful, creative and likeable - all attributes he had failed to find in his previous relationship."

"He's making this up," Cathy protested, holding out her palms. The man in the blue suit indicated for her to be quiet. Cathy crossed her arms and made a face that I assume was meant to be menacing but looked more like she was either pushing out a really huge turd or sucking one back in.

"Yes, Emily certainly was great. We all liked her a lot. She also wrote poems. Good poems though, I believe she was published. Simon was torn when her modelling career demanded she move to Paris for a year. There was talk of him moving with her but he had his successful bowl turning career to think of. The night before Emily left, we held a going away party for her and Simon proposed. She said yes and I have never seen two people so happy. Long distance relationships aren't easy but they had found their soulmates, each other's firefly if you will."

Cathy mouthed the words, "Fuck you."

"Sadly, Emily never made it to Paris. During a six-hour stopover in Indonesia, she decided to take in the sights and while exiting Changhangtang airport, was run over by a rickshaw. It's easy to only look left when you've grown up driving on the right. I was with Simon the evening he received the news that she had passed away. Being here today, we are all aware of the result of his grief, his decision that he couldn't continue without her. I'll miss Simon but I'm glad he found happiness, regardless of the outcome. None of us know how long we have, a night or an eternity, and finding happiness, no matter how brief, is all we can really hope for. I'll finish up with that but please, if we could, a moment's silence for both Simon and Emily."

Everyone bowed their head except Mike, who was shaking his, and Cathy who stood and turned.

"None of that happened," she yelled to the audience.

"Please, miss," the man in the blue suit grabbed her arm, "I'm sorry, but I'm going to have to ask you leave."

Cathy wrestled from his grip and stomped up the aisle, giving Mike the finger as she passed. I heard him say, "Go make me a sandwich, bitch" as she pushed through the door, slamming it with all her strength behind her. It had some kind of shock absorber on it and only made a 'pff' sound. I made my way to my seat and the man in the blue suit took the podium once again.

"Ladies and gentlemen, I apologise for the interruption. David, thank you for sharing those insights into Simon's life with us. It truly is better to have loved and lost than never loved at all. We will now play a song by Simon's favourite band, followed by the committal of the body."

They played a Dave Matthews track, I have no idea which one as they all sound the same. It's the kind of guitar based elevator music that people with beards and beanies listen to while drinking Pabst Blue Ribbon and vaping in their friend Steve's bedroom. They nod along as they flick through mountain biking magazines and discuss CamelBak® water bottles and spoke tightening tools. Thankfully the song was killed halfway through and with a few words, a clank and whirring noises, Simon's coffin lowered into the platform and was gone.

"Is that it?" asked Walter, "we don't get to see it burn?"
"What? No, it goes into a furnace."
"I thought it was going to be a like a fire-pit. That would have been a lot better."
"Yes, we could bring beer and sausages on a stick."
"I didn't know Simon had a hot girlfriend. That's sad about the rickshaw accident."

Jodie took a handful of cheese and an olive toothpicks with her 'for the road' on the way out. Simon's dad shook our hands and thanked us for coming. He told me that he had been stationed in Indonesia during his days in the military and didn't recall an international airport named Changhangtang. He smiled when he said it though.

"Here's to Simon," Mike said, raising his mojito, "he was a fucking idiot at times but he was good at his job."

We raised our glasses and drank, Mike slapped a credit card down and indicated another round to the bartender. Walter dabbed at his tie with a tissue dipped in water. He'd leant across the counter and dragged it through a bowl of salsa. He was pretty upset about it, there was talk about taking it back and pretending it had the stain when he bought it and swapping it for another.

Jennifer raised her glass of Sauvignon Blanc, "He was the only one who ever did his timesheets on time."
"Yes," agreed Jodie, "and vacuumed his office carpet before leaving each day."
We laughed and drank to that.
I raised my Amstel Light, "Here's to the sixteen written and thirty-eight verbal complaints he made against me while we worked together."
"It was a lot more than that," replied Jennifer.
"Was it?"

She nodded and smiled, "Probably closer to a hundred. Most of them were about his pens though."

We drank to a hundred complaints.

Walter raised his vodka & orange, "Here's to Emily."

"Really, Walter?" Mike asked. We drank anyway.

Quick Logo

From: Eugene Buie
Date: Tuesday 26 April 2016 3.38pm
To: David Thorne
Subject: Quick Logo

David,

Hope you are well.

Do you remember the logo you did for the volunteer river cleanup last year? I was wondering if you'd mind doing a similar one for my church youth group. It doesn't need to be anything fancy - I was thinking maybe a dove. I'll leave it up to you though, you're the designer.

The river logo had hands making a circle with a water reed in the middle. Maybe you could just make the reed into a dove? That shouldn't take long.

I have a budget of $300 but that includes 2 banners. It's for a good cause and the group is not-for-profit.

No rush but it would be great to have it before the May services.

Yours, Eugene Buie

From: David Thorne
Date: Tuesday 26 April 2016 4.25pm
To: Eugene Buie
Subject: Re: Quick Logo

Hello Eugene,

Please find attached the revised hand logo incorporating a dove as requested. I feel it symbolises the church/youth relationship perfectly. It's in .eps format so will scale up well for banner usage and I look forward to seeing it in application.

We won't be billing you for this work.

Regards, David

....

From: Eugene Buie
Date: Wednesday 27 April 2016 10.05am
To: David Thorne
Subject: Re: Re: Quick Logo

Thank you, that's perfect.

Yours, Eugene Buie

Hallmark Channel

When Holly channel flicks, she leaves the menu on the screen and scrolls up and down seemingly at random. She also refuses to press the number buttons, only using the up and down arrows, which means if she's on channel 30 and wants to watch 603, she presses the up arrow five-hundred and-ninety times then down another seventeen. She won't even hold the arrow button down in case she misses something.

"What channel are you looking for?"
"I'm just looking."
"All the HD channels are from six-hundred up. You're in the one-hundreds, there's nothing there."
"You never know."
"Yes I do, you've been scrolling through the music channel listings for fifteen minutes."
"So?"
"It's frustrating. Go sit in your car and stare at the stereo if you want to watch music. I sat down to watch television, not watch you scroll through the low-res music channels. Go to the six-hundreds and scroll up from there."
"Fine."
"Should I find something to do while you get there? Maybe carve something out of wood? Just use the number buttons."

"I don't tell you how to use the remote control."

"That's because I use it correctly. If you told me to use it any other way I would ignore your advice due to it being wildly inaccurate."

"Look, I'm in the two-hundreds already."

"Excellent, only four-hundred channels of college football, quilting shows and infomercials for Shark vacuum cleaners to go."

"It's not all football and infomercials... oooh, Hallmark channel. And a movie is just starting."

"You're in the lo-res channels. Hallmark is in HD in the six-hundreds."

"This is fine, I don't care if it's not in HD."

"It's pixelated and only using half the screen. We may as well be watching a cathode ray tube television."

"You're just making up words now. Shhh, the movie's starting."

"We do pay extra for the HD channels."

"Shhh"

"*12 Gifts of Christmas*. This is what we're watching?"

"Shhhhhh."

"In low-res."

"Shhhhhhhhhhh."

"In August."

"Can I just watch the fucking movie, please?"

"Fine."

"Thank you."

"Dreadful choice of typeface for the title. It's like they just didn't give a fuck."

The movie could have been worse but it could have been a lot better. It was basically about a chubby brunette who wears long jackets to hide her thighs and likes painting pictures of Santa. Apparently she's a professional painter but you'd never have guessed because her paintings are terrible. Seriously, the movie is worth watching just for how bad the paintings are. Disappointed that nobody wants to buy her crap paintings of Santa Claus, she takes a job as a professional shopper for a wealthy young advertising executive with great hair. He's too busy to go shopping because he's got to come up with an incredible new advertising pitch for a laptop company but he has time to go ice skating and shit with the chubby brunette. They try on hats and eat muffins and he buys her the ugliest necklace you've ever seen. Then the advertising guy sees her crap painting of Santa and he comes up with the greatest advertising concept ever: Santa holding a laptop. It's fucking genius on so many levels and the laptop company goes apeshit. "Holy fuck!" they say, "That's fucking genius." He's saved the day thanks to the chubby brunette's crap painting and a bit of shocking Photoshop, but the chubby brunette is seriously pissed because he didn't ask to use her crap painting of Santa and as an artist, she painted Santa because she loves Christmas, not for financial gain. Then she's suddenly fine with it and paints a crap painting of the advertising guy with his sister and the old chick from Knott's Landing from memory. The painting is so bad, it makes the Santa painting look like a da Vinci but everyone carries on about it and the advertising guy tells the chubby brunette that she's his Christmas present and they kiss.

"Well that was shit."

"I thought it was nice."

"The movie made no sense. How did she afford a New York apartment when all she did was produce terrible paintings of Santa for a living?"

"That's why she took the job as a professional shopper. To pay the rent."

"Right, but how did she pay the previous month's rent? The entire plot of the movie was based around the fact nobody wanted to buy her crap Santa paintings. Besides, she had a single client who only needed twelve gifts. How is that going to cover the rent?"

"You don't know how much she charged."

"She bought ten scarves, a tiny Christmas tree and a chemistry kit. It was an hour's work."

"Did you even watch the movie? The laptop company cut her a check for using the painting."

"You're missing my point."

"No, I get your point, I just don't care. Maybe she was living off savings and chasing her dream but it didn't pan out and she was getting low on funds. You don't know her."

"If I did, I'd have been honest with her about her painting skills long before her bank balance meant possible eviction. Maybe suggest filling out an Applebee's application or something, you know, just in case there's somehow not a huge market for really bad Santa paintings."

"The paintings were pretty bad."

"Yes, extraordinarily so... maybe that was intentional, so the women who watch this rubbish say to themselves, "That could be me, I too have no talent. I wonder when I'll meet my handsome young advertising executive with great hair?" If the chubby brunette had displayed any skill whatsoever, it would have been far less relatable."

"She wasn't even chubby."

"She was a bit chubby. Which, again, makes her more relatable to the movie's chubby talentless audience."

"You're terrible."

"The movie was terrible, I'm just giving it possible credit for knowing its audience. It's like that show about the fat girl that everyone wants to have to sex with."

"I've no idea what you're taking about."

"That fat girl with the bob on HBO. She wrote a series about how awesome she is and how men want to have sex with her even though she's a huge heifer."

"Lena Dunham? Are you talking about the show *Girls*?"

"That's it. The show is constructed entirely for the purpose of convincing its audience of fat girls that anyone gives a fuck."

"No it isn't."

"It's the heifer version of *Friends*."

"You're an idiot. I know you're joking but do you realise how prejudistic you sound when you say things like that?"

"I'm not being prejudistic, I'm just saying there's nothing worse than a confident fat woman. Except transgender old people of course. Can I have the remote please?"

"No, I'm watching another Hallmark movie."

"*A Boyfriend for Christmas*. Are you serious?"

"Shhhh."

Ben's Shirt

Ben bought a new shirt on the weekend. He wore it to work Monday and flitted gaily in and out of people's offices all morning for us to admire. It looked like any other shirt, perhaps a little shinier because of the cotton/nylon blend, but it wasn't like any other shirt; it was the best shirt in the world. It hadn't been advertised as such but Ben had suspected the shirt was the best shirt in the world the moment he saw it in on the rack. When he tried it on in the changing room, he knew it was. The points on the collar were extra sharp and the collar itself was slightly lower than usual. It also had the second to top button in the correct place; not so high that it looked silly when done up and not so low that it showed chest hair when left undone. It was light blue, bordering on grey-blue. The kind of grey-blue that looks great with either a suit or jeans. He'd worn it tucked in that day but it looked equally as good untucked, it was the perfect length for either. Ninety-five dollars was expensive for a shirt but not for the best shirt in the world. Besides, he'd received ten percent off for signing up for a department store credit card.

"New shirt?" asked Mike.

"Yes," replied Ben, beaming, "it's John Varvatos."

"It's very shiny. You look like you're on your way to a disco."

You Look Like You're

"You look like you're" is Mike's way of saying, "I wouldn't be caught dead in that and here's a thinly disguised insult to explain why." Apparently he's not even aware he's being insulting so maybe it's just something gay men have built in, like the ability to hold their breath under water for a long time. I asked him last week why he couldn't just compliment someone on their attire without using the term, "You look like you're," and he replied, "I've never said that in my life, I'm full of compliments."

As such, I decided to record every time Mike said "You look like you're," over a five day period:

Monday, 10.35am, David's boots.

"New boots?"

"Yes, I ordered them from the Sundance catalogue."

"They look comfy."

"They are."

"You look like you're going for a hike."

"What's that supposed to mean?"

"Nothing, they're very rural, that's all. You know what would go well with those boots?"

"What?"

"A walking staff."

Monday, 12.02pm, Walter's beige cargo shorts

"New cargo shorts, Walter?"

"No, I don't think I've worn these to work before though."

"They're very 'safari'. You look like you're about to wrestle a warthog or point out a giraffe in the distance."

Monday, 3.41pm, Kevin's sweater

"Did your wife knit you a new sweater, Kevin?"

"This? No, it's from JC Penny."

"Cosy. You look like you're about to go crab fishing or take your border collie for a walk across the misty Scottish highlands."

Tuesday, 9.14am, Melissa's yellow dress

"Morning Melissa, is that a new dress?"

"Fairly new."

"It's very floral. You look like you're on your way to a country barn dance or to sell jam at a fair from the back of a pickup truck."

Tuesday, 11.04am, Jennifer's blouse

"New top, Jen?"

"It's a blouse."

"You look like you're about to take a painting class."

"I don't give a fuck what you think, Mike."

"Jesus, learn to take a compliment, Jen."

Wednesday, 9.19am, Jodie's 'Sia' haircut

"Looks like someone's had a haircut."

"Yes, it's a bit short and I've never had bangs but I thought I'd try something a bit more modern."

"It's certainly modern. You look like you're on your way to join the crew of the USS Enterprise. Beam me up, Doctor Spock."

"It's *Mister* Spock, Doctor Spock wrote books on parenting."

"Nobody cares, Space Bob."

Wednesday, 2.24pm, David's black jacket

"Superdry?"

"It's a British clothing brand."

"Yes, I'm aware of the brand, I just didn't know anyone was still wearing it. You look like you're on a night operation as part of a special ops military team."

"Good, that's exactly what I was going for."

"Apart from your physique of course. They'd never let you in. You're too old."

Thursday 9.12am, Melissa's necklace

"That's an interesting necklace, Melissa."

"Thanks, my sister brought it back for me from her trip to Mexico."

"It's Mexican? I would have guessed African. You look like you're on your way to a neighbouring village to be swapped for two cows and a goat-hide water pouch."

Thursday, 4.32pm, Ben's beard

"Are you growing a beard?"

"I thought I'd see how it looks. It hasn't grown in yet."

"Yes, it just looks like you've been camping for a few days. Are you going to grow it all over or just on the chin?"

"All over."

"Good. You look like that stoner guy in Scooby Doo at the moment."

"Shaggy?"

"No, not the dog, the guy that owns the dog."

Friday 9.16am, Walter's grey suit

"Why are you in a suit?"

"I have a funeral to go to at twelve o'clock today."

"You don't own a better suit than that? One that fits? You look like you're on the way to a Salvation Army men's shelter for free soup. Who's the funeral for?"

"My dad. It's one of his suits."

"Right, well grab your phone and let Melissa know we're going out for an hour."

"Why? Where are we going?"

"A store I like. I'm going to buy you a new suit."

Who's Pat?

From: Mike Campbell
Date: Tuesday 15 March 2015 11.09am
To: David Thorne
Subject: Whiteboard

David,

Are you responsible for the drawing of Ben fucking a toaster on the boardroom whiteboard?

Mike

From: David Thorne
Date: Tuesday 15 March 2016 11.13am
To: Mike Campbell
Subject: Re: Whiteboard

Hardly. I drew the image but responsibility for it still being there lies with whoever left a permanent marker amongst the whiteboard ones. Who does that?

David

From: Mike Campbell
Date: Tuesday 15 March 2016 11.18am
To: David Thorne
Subject: Re: Re: Whiteboard

Who draws a picture of someone fucking a toaster on the whiteboard? Permanent or not. Are you 10?

Mike

....

From: David Thorne
Date: Tuesday 15 March 2016 11.21am
To: Mike Campbell
Subject: Re: Re: Re: Whiteboard

There's no way a ten-year-old would display that much attention to detail. I shaded.

David

....

From: Mike Campbell
Date: Tuesday 15 March 2016 11.27am
To: David Thorne
Subject: Re: Re: Re: Re: Whiteboard

Remove it.

Mike

From: Jennifer Haines
Date: Tuesday 15 March 2016 11.40am
To: ALL STAFF
Subject: Formal Notice

Att: All Staff.

Please be aware that producing illustrations depicting coworkers engaged in lewd acts is a form of sexual harassment and workplace bullying. It is a violation of the Employee Workplace Agreement (Section 4, Paragraphs 8 and 9) and will not be tolerated.

This applies to paper drawings, electronic files, whiteboard drawings and all other form of media. Furthermore, the boardroom whiteboard is visible by clients during meetings and is not there for your personal use or amusement.

Also, please ensure only whiteboard markers are used on all whiteboards in future.

Jennifer

....

From: Ben Townsend
Date: Tuesday 15 March 2016 11.48am
To: David Thorne
Subject: Suck shit

Suck shit. And if that's supposed to me it's a pretty sad reflection of your drawing skills because nobody would ever be able to tell.

From: David Thorne
Date: Tuesday 15 March 2016 11.51am
To: Ben Townsend
Subject: Re: Suck shit

The fedora is kind of a giveaway, Ben. Nobody else has worn one since 2011.

....

From: Ben Townsend
Date: Tuesday 15 March 2016 11.56am
To: David Thorne
Subject: Re: Re: Suck shit

Like you know fashion. 1992 called, it wants its hair back.

....

From: David Thorne
Date: Tuesday 15 March 2016 11.59am
To: Ben Townsend
Subject: Re: Re: Re: Suck shit

1766 also called. Your wooden teeth are due for a scraping.

....

From: Ben Townsend
Date: Tuesday 15 March 2016 12.03pm
To: David Thorne
Subject: Re: Re: Re: Re: Suck shit

That doesn't even make any sense. You did the joke wrong.

From: David Thorne
Date: Tuesday 15 March 2016 12.11pm
To: Ben Townsend
Subject: Re: Re: Re: Re: Re: Suck shit

The YMCA called. Your racquetball court is confirmed for 4PM.

....

From: Ben Townsend
Date: Tuesday 15 March 2016 12.15pm
To: David Thorne
Subject: Re: Re: Re: Re: Re: Re: Suck shit

Stop listening to my calls.

....

From: Walter Bowers
Date: Tuesday 15 March 2016 12.21pm
To: David Thorne
Subject: No Subject

Did you the whiteboard?

....

From: David Thorne
Date: Tuesday 15 March 2016 12.24pm
To: Walter Bowers
Subject: Re: No Subject

Can I buy a verb please, Pat?

From: Mike Campbell
Date: Tuesday 15 March 2016 12.31pm
To: David Thorne
Subject: Meeting

David,

I have a meeting in the boardroom at 2. I want the drawing removed before then please.

Mike

....

From: David Thorne
Date: Tuesday 15 March 2016 12.36pm
To: Mike Campbell
Subject: Re: Meeting

I'm not sure how. I attempted to remove the marker with Windex and a scourer but it took off more surface than ink. Ben's hat is a bit lighter now though if that helps.

David

....

From: Mike Campbell
Date: Tuesday 15 March 2016 12.47pm
To: David Thorne
Subject: Re: Re: Meeting

No, it doesn't. Did you try nail polish remover?

Mike

From: David Thorne
Date: Tuesday 15 March 2016 12.50pm
To: Melissa Peters
Subject: Acetone

Melissa,

Do we have any nail polish remover? Someone left a permanent marker amongst the boardroom whiteboard markers and I need to remove a drawing of Ben having sex with a toaster.

David

....

From: Melissa Peters
Date: Tuesday 15 March 2016 12.59pm
To: David Thorne
Subject: Re: Acetone

You can't use nail polish remover. It will damage the whiteboard. You just have to rub a whiteboard marker tip over the permanent marker and it will come straight off.

Do you want me to do it for you?

....

From: David Thorne
Date: Tuesday 15 March 2016 1.03pm
To: Melissa Peters
Subject: Re: Re: Acetone

Yes please.

From: David Thorne
Date: Tuesday 15 March 2016 1.05pm
To: Mike Campbell
Subject: Re: Re: Re: Meeting

Mike,

I've spoken with Melissa. She says we can't use nail polish remover as it will damage the whiteboard. We're probably just going to have to live with it.

David

....

From: Mike Campbell
Date: Tuesday 15 March 2016 1.17pm
To: David Thorne
Subject: Re: Re: Re: Re: Meeting

No we wont. I don't give a fuck if you have to use sandpaper, I want the drawing removed before 2.

Mike

....

From: David Thorne
Date: Tuesday 15 March 2016 1.21pm
To: Mike Campbell
Subject: Re: Re: Re: Re: Re: Meeting

If you stand with your back against the whiteboard during the meeting, no-one will even see it.

David

From: Mike Campbell
Date: Tuesday 15 March 2016 1.27pm
To: David Thorne
Subject: Re: Re: Re: Re: Re: Re: Meeting

Is that meant to be a joke? Why would I be standing with my back against the whiteboard for the whole meeting?

Mike

....

From: David Thorne
Date: Tuesday 15 March 2016 1.40pm
To: Mike Campbell
Subject: Re: Re: Re: Re: Re: Re: Re: Meeting

There's any number of reasons why you might be standing with your back against the whiteboard. If anyone asks, tell them you have an itchy back and wiggle a bit while making pleasurable sounds. Tell them it's shingles. Apparently if you've ever had the measles then the shingles virus is already inside of you.

Alternatively, I could send Ben down to stand there. He's not busy at the moment. I overheard him tell somebody on the phone that he's bored and considering leaving early to play racquetball. I realise he's shorter than the height of the drawing but he could stand on a box. You can tell the client that he's on work experience and only there to observe.

Should I send him down at 2 or a bit before to practice?

David

From: Mike Campbell
Date: Tuesday 15 March 2016 1.48pm
To: David Thorne
Subject: Re: Re: Re: Re: Re: Re: Re: Re: Meeting

Work out some way to remove the drawing or cover it up within the next 10 minutes please.

And yes, you can send Ben down. The only reason I'm having this meeting is because we've blown the deadline and if he's got time to fuck off and play racquetball, he can explain to the client why he hasn't even written the copy yet.

Mike

....

From: David Thorne
Date: Tuesday 15 March 2016 2.05pm
To: Ben Townsend
Subject: New product discussion

Ben,

Mike has asked that you be in the 2 o'clock meeting.

....

From: Ben Townsend
Date: Tuesday 15 March 2016 2.08pm
To: David Thorne
Subject: Re: New product discussion

What for? Who's it with? That meeting has already started.

From: David Thorne
Date: Tuesday 15 March 2016 2.11pm
To: Ben Townsend
Subject: Re: Re: New product discussion

Well you'd better get down there then. Have you heard of a company called Babolat? Apparently they make sporting gear or something.

Mike said to take down your racquetball equipment so they can get an idea of product dimensions.

....

From: Ben Townsend
Date: Tuesday 15 March 2016 2.13pm
To: David Thorne
Subject: Re: Re: Re: New product discussion

Alright.

....

From: Ben Townsend
Date: Tuesday 15 March 2016 2.45pm
To: David Thorne
Subject: Fuck you

Fucking liar.

From: David Thorne
Date: Tuesday 15 March 2016 2.48pm
To: Ben Townsend
Subject: Re: Fuck you

1070 called, it's still waiting on the Bayeux Tapestry copy.

....

From: Walter Bowers
Date: Tuesday 15 March 2016 3.34pm
To: David Thorne
Subject: Re: Re: No Subject

Who's Pat?

Mrs Gillespie

I saw my father eating out Mrs Gillespie when I was seven. She was our next door neighbour. Her husband, Mr Gillespie, often came over to our house to drink beer and watch cricket with my father. He called me 'Champ' and once welded a broken frame on my bike. I'd ridden home from school after recess that day because Andrew Fitzgerald hit me in the back of my head with a metal sprinkler; I'd cried in front of several classmates and couldn't face them at the next lesson. My mother and father both worked and I knew nobody would be home so I let myself in the back door and made my way towards the kitchen to get a snack. Back then, before my father moved out, there were always snacks in the fridge. Mrs Gillespie was on the L-shaped kitchen counter, one foot on the sink and the other on the breakfast bar, her head back, dress up around her waist, and underpants on the kitchen floor. My father was on his knees, facing away from me with his head between her legs.

A few days earlier, I'd been playing barefooted on the grass in the backyard and stepped on a bee. My father carried me inside, placed me on the kitchen counter with my foot up, and removed the stinger with a pair of tweezers.

"Did Mrs Gillespie get stung by a bee?" I asked.

Mrs Gillespie screamed, slamming her legs together and pulling her dress down. My father pushed himself from her clenched thighs, fell backwards onto the kitchen tiles and stared up at me with his mouth and eyes wide open. Mrs Gillespie slid down from the counter, collected her underwear and ran out.

He could have lied, convinced me that what I saw was not worth mentioning to my mother, I wouldn't have known better. I hadn't received 'the talk' and my only knowledge about such things came from my cousin Darryl who told me babies were shot out of t-shirt guns at concerts. Even a bribe might have worked. Instead, I guess my father decided to pre-empt being dobbed on and come clean to my mother.

My older sister Leith and I stayed with our Auntie Phyllis that night. She picked us up from the house around four o'clock - an hour or so before my mother usually got home - and we went to see *Superman* at the cinema. I wasn't a fan of staying at my auntie's house because she made us do chores. Not small chores like changing the kitty litter or taking the trash out; she had us re-tile her bathroom and sand & stain floorboards. Once, she made me re-concrete loose chimney bricks on her roof. Worse than that, was the fact that she didn't own a television. Not because she was poor, but because she chose not to. This made no sense as it meant she missed out on seeing *The Six Million Dollar Man*, the best television show ever made. Instead of watching television, we played card games and charades.

"First word... The."

"Second word... fingers? No? ... counting? No? Oh, six?"

"mmhmm"

"Okay, third word... sounds like... dancing? No? Electric shock? No? Wriggling? No? I give up."

"I was jiggling!"

"Why didn't you just nod and tap your nose when I said wriggling then? Wriggling rhymes with jiggling."

"Oh yeah."

"The six jiggling what?"

"No, jiggling 'sounds like' million."

"*The Six Million Dollar Man*?"

"Yes!"

"Jiggling doesn't sound anything like million."

"It does if you say it like 'jigilin.'"

Our house felt different when we returned the next day. Usually we ate dinner in front of the television in the living room. My sister and I would argue about staying up past our bedtimes. That evening, however, we ate a Kentucky Fried Chicken family bucket meal at the kitchen table. Nobody spoke and halfway through the meal, my mother started crying and slammed a glass of Coke down on the table, hard enough to smash it and cut her hand. My father said nothing, my mother wrapped a teatowel around her hand and kept eating. My sister glanced at me, I looked down - I didn't want to rock the boat as there were more drumsticks. There was a knock on the door and my sister and I were told to go to our rooms and stay there.

I could hear them shouting from beneath the open bathroom window that overlooked our backyard. I climbed onto the edge of the bath tub and peeked out. Mr and Mrs Gillespie sat on a swinging chair and my parents at a cast-iron patio set. My mother had made coffee for everyone in her new Bodum® glass coffee press - it had been her Christmas present that year from my father even though she only drank tea.

For Christmas the previous year, my father bought my mother a lambswool steering wheel cover for her car but it was the wrong size so he put it on his steering wheel. The year before that, he gave her a set of plastic picnic tumblers with his favourite football team's logo on them and a year's subscription to Sports Illustrated. For her birthday one year, he blindfolded my mother and led her outside to reveal a ride-on lawnmower he had bought himself. We only had a quarter-acre block and most of the yard was concrete because my parents had bought the house from a Greek family. The first thing they did when we moved in was remove a twelve-foot concrete fountain shaped like a rearing horse from the front yard. They had to bring in a crane. The ride-on mower cut my father's gardening time down dramatically though, it took less than a minute to complete the small patch of lawn in the backyard and that included driving the mower out of the shed and putting it back. He let me have a go on it once but I ran over a concrete gnome and wasn't allowed near it after that. I went a year without pocket-money to pay for new blades.

It was the mature thing to do I suppose, to sit down and discuss the situation over coffee like adults, they were neighbours after all. Our family and the Gillespie's had even gone camping together once. We camped on the edge of the Murray River, an hour's drive from the village of Adelaide, during an Australia Day* long weekend. After setting up camp and building a fire, my father and Mr Gillespie drank a three day supply of beer and Mrs Gillespie had to drive Mr Gillespie to the hospital for alcohol poisoning. My father went with them because he fell over one of those bits of rope that hold the tents up and cut his chin open on a camp stove. He got four stitches. When they got back that evening, with more beer, they started drinking again and eventually fell asleep in their camping chairs. My mother and Mrs Gillespie left them there. In the morning, their faces and arms were covered in tens of thousands of mosquito bites so they spent the day drinking at the water's edge covered in mud. There wasn't much for me to do apart from paddle around in an inflatable raft but my father and Mr Gillespie popped it when they both tried to get in while drunk. They tried fixing it with duct tape but it didn't hold air so I spent two days whacking things with a stick and asking when we were leaving.

---

* *Australia Day is similar to the 4th of July in the United States but involves far less fucking around with fireworks and far more beer. There's a bit of flag waving but not as enthusiastically as the American holiday because Australia never had the balls to tell England to fuck off and is still a colony. It celebrates the day some Pommy git sailed in, massacred the locals, and said, "This is mine," so it's more like Columbus Day actually. There's mattress sales and the post office is closed.*

"And I want my barbecue tongs back," shouted Mr Gillespie, "You've had them since we went camping."

"That's fine," replied my father, "but could you keep your voice down, please? I'm sure we can discuss this like adults without resorting to yelling."

"That's easy for you to say," replied Mr Gillespie, "how about I fuck your wife four or five times and we'll see how calm you are about it."

"Okay, now you're just being ridiculous."

"Oh, *I'm* ridiculous? You're the one cheating on your wife, you sad fucking wanker."

My mother leaned forward, put her face in her hands and sobbed. My father reached across the table and rubbed her back, she swiped his hand away with disgust.

"Don't touch me," she spat.

"Perhaps this wasn't a good idea," my father said.

"Which part?" asked Mr Gillespie, "Fucking my wife or wanting to sit down to chat about it afterwards? What exactly did you think was going to happen? That I'd say, "That's fine, why don't you give her one up the arse, she likes that?""

"No I don't," said Mrs Gillespie.

"Yes you do, don't lie, you cheap fucking whore. You fucking love it."

"Did you fuck her up the arse?" my mother asked my father.

"No," he replied.

"I bet you did," she pointed a finger at my father and said to Mr Gillespie, "He sticks his finger in my arse when we're having sex all the time."

I understood at that moment what they were talking about. The word 'fuck' had little reference apart from being a word you got your mouth washed out with soap for using, but I knew the word sex. My father had had sex with Mrs Gillespie. Four or five times apparently. And, having sex involved sticking your finger in people's bums. That must have been what he was doing in the kitchen I realised, looking at her bum to see where to stick his finger in. I decided that evening that I was never going to have sex.

Mr Gillespie turned to his wife, "Did he stick his finger up your arse while he fucked you?"

She looked down into her coffee.

"I want to know."

Mrs Gillespie actually nodded.

"Look," my father said, "The details aren't important, what matters is how we dea..."

"I thought you were my friend," said Mr Gillespie.

"I am."

"Friend's don't fuck their friend's wives."

"Well, we were never *good* friends," my father said, "we just watched the cricket toge..."

Mr Gillespie leapt up and punched my father.

It was a proper punch; there was enough hurt and anger behind it to break his jaw. My father flopped back in his chair for a second or two, his eyes rolling back in his head. He came to, clumsily tried to get up. Mr Gillespie punched him again, breaking his nose.

My mother screamed as blood spurted like a fountain, it covered the front of my father's favourite white and blue striped tennis shirt and splashed across the concrete like someone had flicked a paint brush. My father raised a hand to his face, his other up in defence. Mr Gillespie raised his fist again.

"Stop!" I yelled.

Mr Gillespie froze, they all stared up at me in the bathroom window. My father looked away, my mother put her head back in her hands and wailed. Mr Gillespie stepped back, grabbed his wife firmly by the arm and pulled her off the swinging chair. Before they left through the side gate, he turned and looked up at me. "Your father," he said, "is not a good man. It's good you saw this."

Perhaps it was. I've never even had the inclination to cheat on anyone in my life and during the times I've been single, have never slept with someone that I knew was in a relationship. There was one discrepancy in the first year of high school when I lent Emma Jenkins a pen in history and was chased after school by Andrew Fitzgerald, but they weren't really seeing each other. Andrew said they were but Emma denied it and said the only boy she liked was Uncle Jesse from Full House. Andrew didn't catch me, I dove under a tarpaulin covering firewood in someone's front yard and heard him run past. That was the first time I was ever bitten by a snake. It wasn't venomous but my arm swelled up a bit.

My father drove himself to the hospital. He may have indicated to my mother that he'd like her to drive him but I doubt she was having a bar of it. She didn't drive stick anyway and my father had refused to step foot in my mother's car since he'd undergone hypnosis to give up smoking earlier that year. He was instructed, while under, that cigarette smoke would, from that point on, smell like rancid meat. It took surprisingly well so there might be something to the whole hypnosis thing. My mother smoked in her Mini Morris and he said it smelt like it was full of dead cats. He'd had to catch a taxi home from the hypnosis session because his own car smelled the same. He traded it in on a new car and whenever we went on family drives, he made my mother shower and change clothes before she was allowed in. He once tried to convince her to wear one of those scented things shaped like a pine tree around her wrist but she wasn't keen on that so he kept a can of disinfectant spray in the centre console and would spray it around occasionally while driving. Once, he sprayed her hair.

He was gone for three days and my mother spent most of that time in her bedroom. When I put my ear against her closed door, I heard her sobbing and talking to herself, mainly asking questions. My sister made tomato soup for dinner the first night and our aunty Phyllis picked us up to stay at her house the following evening. I mended her fence and cleaned out gutters while my sister steamed floral wallpaper off the dining room walls. Later, we sponge painted it as Phyllis was going for a Mexican cantina theme.

The next time I saw I my father, his nose was in plaster and his jaw was wired. Though he hadn't been punched in the eyes, they were black and swollen, the left almost closed. He knocked on my bedroom door and handed me a notebook that said, "I'm sorry."

"That's okay," I said, I wasn't even sure what he was apologising to me for, "Does your nose hurt?"

He took back the notebook and wrote, "Yes."

"You could have just nodded," I said, "Is Mum angry at you?"

He nodded.

"Just show her the note that says 'I'm sorry.'"

He flipped the page on the notebook and wrote, "Clean your room. It looks like a bomb went off in here."

There's a Japanese art called Kintsukuroi which consists of repairing broken bowls and dishes with lacquer mixed with powdered gold. As a philosophy, it treats breakage and repair as part of the history of an object, rather than something to disguise. Some of the repaired bowls and dishes look nice and some turn out a bit dodgy. It depends on the degree of skill of course, whether the gold lacquer was slopped on with a brush or blended perfectly, but also on if the dish was worth repairing in the first place. Some dishes are special dishes, like a limited edition Charles & Diana commemorative wedding dish, while other dishes are just dishes. Our dishes get thrown out if they get chipped or broken, replaced when we realise we only have two left. There's no point wasting gold lacquer when we can get a Färgrik 18-piece dinnerware set from IKEA for $19.99.

I didn't see my father for a month, then he came to dinner one night and brought us all gifts. My sister received a press-on nail kit and I got a Lite-Brite set. For those not familiar with the Lite-Brite, it's basically a board and coloured translucent pegs. You stick the pegs in the board and flick a switch and a light in the board shines through the pegs. I'm not really sure what the point of it was. He bought my mother a gold bracelet but she didn't put it on. Years later, after the divorce, she tried to sell it but it turned out to be only plated and worth about ten dollars. My father came to dinner the next few nights as well, then stayed after dinner to watch television, then stayed the night, then everything somehow went back to normal. I guess they talked and promises were made. For a while it was better than normal, we went to the movies and the zoo and even on a family cruise. While aboard the cruise, my mother caught Legionnaires' disease from a contaminated spa filter and ended up spending three weeks in hospital. My father visited her a couple of times and took us once; we waved to her through a transparent plastic tent. After she was released from hospital, she had to stay in bed for another few weeks so my father took time off work to pick her up and take her to my auntie Phyllis's house. The cruise company refunded the fare and my parents bought a waterbed with the money. They put up with it for about two weeks before moving their old mattress back in from the garage. Mr and Mrs Gillespie divorced and sold their house. The couple who bought it, Mr and Mrs Williams, had two bassett hounds and a daughter named Tracy.

Tracy was a few years older than me, eleven or twelve, and she and my sister instantly became friends. Tracy often slept at our house and my sister and her would arrange blankets and pillows on our large modular sofa in the living area. They'd stay up late watching movies and doing whatever thirteen-year-old girls do at sleepovers. As a nine-year-old boy, I wasn't welcome to join and I didn't care; I was caught spying on them once and they'd crimped my hair. I awoke one night, thirsty, and made my way to the kitchen to get a drink. It was late, past twelve o'clock, and my parents had long gone to bed. My sister was snoring softly on the sofa but Tracy was awake. She called me in and asked if I wanted to watch the movie *Every Which Way But Loose* with her. Not being one to turn down the chance to stay up late and watch television, I made myself comfy beside her. At some point, Tracy asked if I'd ever kissed a girl. When I admitted I hadn't, she offered to show me how. It was my first kiss and the first time a girl ever touched my penis. I won't go into graphic detail but it was a 'show me yours and I'll show you mine' kind of thing. Tracy laid back and lifted her knees, pulling her pyjama pants around her thighs.

"Stick your finger in," she said.
"No," I replied, horrified.
"Just do it," she demanded angrily, "but lick your finger first so its got spit on it."
"What for?"
"So it goes in easier."
I licked my finger and shoved it up her bum.

My sister woke when Tracy yelled and my mother got up to see what the commotion was about. She told me to stop annoying the girls, slapped me across the ear, and sent me back to my room. As I lay in the dark sobbing, my ear throbbing, I lifted my finger, gave it a sniff, and quickly pulled it away again. It made no sense, why would people like this?

When I was in sixth grade, a classmate named Bradley McPherson told a group of us that he had fingered Caitlyn Rivers behind the incinerator near the soccer field. There was a rumour going around that Caitlyn had once shown her nipples in exchange for a packet of cheese and onion chips, so it was a believable story.

"Did she make you?" I asked.
"No," Bradley replied, "I wanted to."
"Oh my god, why?"
"Cause it feels nice. It's warm and slippery in there."
"That's disgusting. Did you wash your finger afterwards?"
"No, do you want to smell it?"
"Hell no."

The others in the group took Bradley up on his offer which I found inexplicable. I watched in disbelief as they clambered for their turn at a whiff, a couple of them actually going in for seconds. One of the boys, a chubby redhead named Dennis, tried wiping his finger against Bradley's to transfer the smell.

That weekend, I slept over my friend Dominic's house and I told him about Bradley sticking his finger in Caitlyn's bum.

"Why would anyone want to do that?" Dominic asked.

"That's what I'm saying."

"Wouldn't it stink?"

"Yes," I answered, relaying the story of the time Tracy Williams had me do it.

"Maybe, " he postulated, "it's not for the person that sticks their finger in. Maybe its just for the person who gets the finger up their bum. Maybe it only feels nice to *them* and you're just doing them a favor."

"Maybe," I agreed, "That makes more sense. Like how it doesn't feel that great to scratch someone's back but when they scratch your back, it's pretty nice."

"Exactly, and like washing someone's hair."

"How is that like it?"

"It's not that fun to wash someone else's hair but when the hairdresser washes your hair, it feels really nice."

"Who's hair do you wash?"

"My grandma's."

"She can't wash her own hair?"

"I don't mind doing it. Let's test it, you stick your finger in my bum and I'll tell you if it feels nice."

"No way, how come I have to be the one sticking his finger in?"

"Fine," conceded Dominic, "I'll stick my finger in your bum then."

"Alright."

It hadn't felt nice, regardless of the amount of spit. I was on all fours with my pants down and his finger half way in when Dominic's mother walked in. She drove me home and Dominic and I weren't allowed to hang out with each other after that.

We had sex education class the next year, which cleared up the misconception. After covering the reproductive system, our teacher, Mr Henderson, asked students to call out alternative names for having sex and wrote them on the blackboard. It got some laughs, which was its intention. Being Australian, 'rooting' was at the top of the list. Mr Henderson wiped the board clean.

"Okay," he said, "before the male and female have sexual intercourse, or 'root', they engage in an activity known as foreplay. This stimulates and prepares the body, and the mind, for intercourse. Can someone give me an example of foreplay?"

I raised my hand.

There was some debate as to whether licking your finger and sticking it in someone's bum was considered foreplay or intercourse, but Mr Henderson added it to the list along with kissing, touching, and having a bath together.

Eskimo Day

Seb paused his game of *War of the Monsters* and yelled into the kitchen, "Oh yeah, I almost forgot, tomorrow's Eskimo day at school."
He was five and it was way past his bedtime.
"What the fuck is Eskimo Day?" I yelled back.
"Everyone has to dress like an Eskimo."
"Oh my god, Seb. It's almost ten o'clock."

We pulled it off but it was past three in the morning before we climbed into our beds. A large faux-fur blanket had been sacrificed to create the overshirt, I cut out two T shapes and hand sewed them together. A half circle of the same blanket stitched to the neck line formed a fur hood. I made the fur boots the same way, hand stitching curved tubes that he could he could pull over his shoes. For his spear, I removed the shower curtain rod and attached a bread knife to it with duct tape. It had all come together and wasn't half bad.

We were tired but made it to his school the next morning no later than our usual lateness, I walked him into his class wearing his outfit. It was 'Excursion Day' and everyone was dressed to go to a local quarry to learn about fossils. There was a permission slip in the bottom of his schoolbag that stated, 'please dress appropriately'.

The Peckish Activities

From: David Thorne
Date: Thursday 19 May 2016 2.05pm
To: Steven Semmens
Subject: Plagiarism

Dear Steven,

It was bought to my attention today that you have been re-posting articles from my website. As audience-reach relies largely on people like yourself sharing these articles with others, regardless of whether the original source is credited or not, I appreciate you doing so.

If, however, you could refrain from changing my name in the articles to yours and telling everyone you wrote them, I would appreciate that more.

Regards, David

....

From: Steven Semmens
Date: Thursday 19 May 2016 3.41pm
To: David Thorne
Subject: Re: Plagiarism

You don't own words.

From: David Thorne
Date: Thursday 19 May 2016 4.06pm
To: Steven Semmens
Subject: Re: Re: Plagiarism

Dear Steven,

Perhaps not individual ones, but when placed next to each-other to form sentences, they become attributable. Your response to one of your Facebook friends asking, "Did you really try to pay your bill with a drawing of a seven-legged spider Steven?" with, "Yeah, brilliant ay, I'm right mad sometimes!" infers self attribution. While most people avoid outright plagiarism due to self respect, respect for the original author, or fear of being called out and looking like a dickhead, you appear to be free of such constraints.

Having had a quick glance at your Facebook friend list, I understand that it is unlikely anyone you know has ever read a book or visited a website containing more than pictures, but surely at some point one of them has to ask, "How is that guy from Swansea - you know, the one that looks like a burn victim - formulating and posting three articles a day? I was under the impression he had some form of severe intellectual disability but apparently he has also written a book about women's archery called *The Peckish Activities* and several volumes about a magical boy named Barry."

Regards, David

From: Steven Semmens
Date: Thursday 19 May 2016 4.14pm
To: David Thorne
Subject: Re: Re: Re: Plagiarism

Who asked you to look at what i was posting? I changed the stories so it is only half your text. You're not Steven King nobody I know has even heard of you.

From: David Thorne
Date: Thursday 19 May 2016 4.23pm
To: Steven Semmens
Subject: Re: Re: Re: Re: Plagiarism

Dear Steven,

Firstly, I doubt Mr King's work being well known would prove any obstacle to you releasing your own novel titled *Christina, the Self-Healing Vauxhall Nova* and despite the absence of memorable prom-night moments, sewer clowns or magic fog in my 'writings', you obviously found them worthy enough to appropriate and claim as your own.

Secondly, changing my name to yours and the single line "a crowd gathered, wide eyed and eager" to "some fat english bastards gorped" is hardly 'half' the text.'

Regards, David

From: Steven Semmens
Date: Thursday 19 May 2016 4.37pm
To: David Thorne
Subject: Re: Re: Re: Re: Re: Plagiarism

Changed more than that I added bits too to make the stories a lot better.

....

From: David Thorne
Date: Thursday 19 May 2016 4.50pm
To: Steven Semmens
Subject: Re: Re: Re: Re: Re: Re: Plagiarism

Dear Steven,

Yes, I noticed the additional copy. Particularly paragraph two of your viral email exchange titled *Missing Missy* where you replied to Shannon's request for help in finding her missing cat with:

"Ay Shannon, well yer cats prolly fucked then aint it? One of them Easties prolly ate it. You know what they're like they'd prolly eat a warm turd if they was hungry enough."

In this instance, I actually appreciate you changing my name to yours.

Regards, David

From: Steven Semmens
Date: Thursday 19 May 2016 5.04pm
To: David Thorne
Subject: Re: Re: Re: Re: Re: Re: Re: Plagiarism

I'm not taking them down.

From: David Thorne
Date: Thursday 19 May 2016 5.16pm
To: Steven Semmens
Subject: Re: Re: Re: Re: Re: Re: Re: Re: Plagiarism

Nobody's asking you to, Steven. I'm just calling you out for being a twat.

I look forward to reading more of your work in your upcoming novels, *The Internet is an Empty Lot to Muck About In*, *Look Evelyn, Duck Dynasty Wiper Blades. We Should Shoplift a Pair*, and *That's Not How You Wash a Pit Bull terrier*.

Regards, David

From: Steven Semmens
Date: Thursday 19 May 2016 5.22pm
To: David Thorne
Subject: Re: Re: Re: Re: Re: Re: Re: Re: Re: Plagiarism

Your the twat.

From: David Thorne
Date: Thursday 19 May 2016 5.24pm
To: Steven Semmens
Subject: Re: Re: Re: Re: Re: Re: Re: Re: Re: Re: Plagiarism

*you're the twat.

....

From: Steven Semmens
Date: Thursday 19 May 2016 5.29pm
To: David Thorne
Subject: Re: Re: Re: Re: Re: Re: Re: Re: Re: Re: Re: Plagiarism

Real original.

Robert the Telemarketing Raccoon

Something had been in the wheelie bins. They were tipped over and torn bags were strewn across the yard. A garbage bag was all the way at the end of our driveway, the contents spilled onto the road for all the neighbours to see. It was lucky we hadn't thrown out a huge dildo or something as our neighbours are huge gossips. I bought a new leaf blower recently and a few days later, the lady at the post office asked me what Mph* it was rated at. It's to be expected in a small village though, when the most exciting thing locals have to look forward to is Gwen McKinnley's annual quilt sale at her 'dead people's glassware and blankets' store, someone buying a shovel, pants, or leaf blower makes front page news.

"Hello, Mr Thorne? Brent Finnegan here, Harrisonburg News, just following up on a report we received that you have a new leaf blower. Can you confirm this?"
"Er, yes."
"Fantastic. Very exciting. What Mph is it rated at?"

---

* *251 Mph for those wondering. I didn't actually need a new leaf blower but my neighbour Carl just bought a new one and seemed pretty pleased with it so I bought a better one than his to diminish his satisfaction. Mine has straps so you can wear it like a big backpack. Carl has to carry his like a peasant. I waited to use my leaf blower until Carl used his one afternoon and waved when he looked over. He turned his off and went inside so it was totally worth the five-hundred dollars.*

I re-bagged the garbage, gagging a few times as I'm not a huge fan of raw chicken that's been in the sun for three or four days. There was also a ripped open bag of dog vomit as, a few days before, our dog Laika worked out how to open her food storage bin and ate a month's worth of food in the time it took me to have a shower. She weighs sixty pounds and it was sixty pounds of dog food so I'm not sure how that's even possible. I stepped out of the bathroom in bare feet and into the first pile of vomit - I'd heard her retching a bit while I was in the shower but it's one of her regular annoying noises so I'd ignored it; she's a fat pig so spends ninety-percent of her time sighing, snorting, grunting, making a weird 'haphaaar' noise, and farting. The wet, warm pile, around thirty-pounds of regurgitated meaty bites, came just above my ankle. It was similar to how I imagine putting your foot into a bucket of warm slugs might feel. At the sound of more retching, I hopped quickly down the hallway just in time to witness what looked like Laika giving birth to a huge thirty-pound alien snake through her mouth. Luckily, she'd managed to make it from the hallway to the living room rug for the second half.

The bins were tipped over again the next night. I walked around picking up and rebagging chicken, vomit, and the Indian takeaway we'd had the night before. My neighbour Carl came outside to see what I was doing and, realising I'd be a while, rushed back inside to grab his budget leaf blower and do his yard before I had the chance to grab mine.

I decided to use the leaf blower to blow the strewn garbage into a pile, which is how we ended up with chicken, vomit and indian takeaway all over our siding. Luckily, Carl had purchased a new pressure washer six months earlier so I'd ordered a better one. I hadn't been able to make out the PSI rating on his washer, even through binoculars, so I'd just ordered the highest PSI available. It's a supercharged V8 with cold air intake and will strip paint from a fence twenty feet away. I shot Seb with it as a joke the day I got it but forgot he had no sense of humour. He only required twelve stitches but the way he still carries on about it, you'd have thought his left nipple had been completely ripped off. Some people just need to play the martyr.

I placed the wheelie bins on our back deck instead of their usual place by the basement door as the back deck is fenced off. That evening, after pausing *Shark Tank* to get a snack from the kitchen, I heard a noise from the back deck and flicked on the back light.

"Holly, there's a raccoon on the back deck."
"Really? What's it doing?"
"Eating tika masala and naan."

He ran when I opened the back door but stopped a few dozen feet away. I picked up his naan and threw it to him. It dropped a few feet short but he walked over and took it, tearing off small pieces with tiny human-like hands and eating them gingerly while watching me clean up the mess.

I bought latches for the bins the next day. It must be a common problem in the area as the assistant at Lowe's knew what aisle they were in. They were more of a strap than a latch but did the trick; the raccoon returned around ten o'clock that evening and couldn't get into the bins. I heard the first get tipped over, watched as he tipped the second and clawed desperately to get the lid off. He gave up after about ten minutes and sat on the fence staring through the glass door at me. We'd had lasagna that night for dinner and there was still some left so I cut him a slice and put it on a plate. Thinking lasagna might not be the healthiest of meals for a raccoon, I added an apple and placed the plate outside.

He had pizza the following night. I ordered him a small deep pan margarita with pineapple. For dessert, he had half a cantaloupe lightly sprinkled with sugar and a dollop of ice cream.

He came early the third night, it was still dusk when I noticed him waiting patiently outside the back door. His roasted jacket potato hadn't had time to cool so I cut it open and blew on it for a bit before smothering it with sour cream, shredded cheese and coleslaw. He backed up when I opened the door to give it to him but he didn't run away. I'd baked carrot cake for dessert and served it still warm in a bowl with two large scoops of ice cream and fresh strawberries. He didn't back up when I placed the bowl on the deck and if I'd been inclined to do so, I could probably have reached out and patted his fur.

"What should we name him?" asked Holly.

"We've had this conversation before," I answered, "when you give something a name it's harder to say goodbye to it."

"It made no difference with Squirrel."

"That's true."

"And besides, you're already calling him 'he' instead of 'it.'"

"Fine, name him then."

"Okay, I'll call him Robert."

"Really?"

"What's wrong with the name Robert?"

"Nothing if you're a mattress salesman. It's an odd name for a raccoon though."

"I know a Robert and he's not a mattress salesman. He's a sales rep for the local radio station."

"How is that any better?"

"Fine, you name him then."

"No, you've already named him. We're stuck with Robert now. Robert the telemarketing raccoon. He'll take twenty-percent off if you book ten radio spots and throw in a pillow-top mattress."

On the fourth night, after giving Robert his cauliflower crepes with sautéed asparagus and grilled cheese topping, I accidentally left the back door slightly ajar when I headed back to the kitchen to get his crème brûlée. I'd put it in the refrigerator a half hour earlier to cool down and when I collected it and closed the refrigerator door, I saw Robert five or six feet from me, inside the house, waiting expectantly. I put the crème brûlée on the floor, near the dog's food bowls, and took a step back. He approached without reservation and dug in, looking up at me as he scooped up handfuls of caramel and custard and ate it with fervour. I considered reaching down slowly and patting him then, he may have let me and the relationship would have been sealed, but I didn't get the chance to try. As Robert neared the bottom of his bowl, scraping custard from the sides, he pushed the bowl forward and it clinked against Laika's ceramic food bowl.

Up until that point, our dogs hadn't paid any attention to Robert. I'm not sure they'd even seen him. He'd stayed outside and moved slowly, usually in the dark. Hearing the clink of food bowls however, Laika and Banksy waddled into the kitchen to investigate the possibility of a second dinner at the exact same moment Holly yelled, "Who left the back door open?" and slammed it shut.

We had to repaint the kitchen, hallway and living room walls. The blood had even splattered the ceiling in several places and it was difficult to colour match so I ended up having to paint all of it. I'll never bitch about painting walls again after having to do ceilings. Our leather couch had to be replaced, as did most of the window coverings, an area rug, two lamps and a Herman Miller Noguchi coffee table. The glass on a Noguchi coffee table weighs 165 pounds and when the base went with Robert underneath, it killed him almost instantly. As he died, a paw sticking out from beneath the glass wiggled a bit as if he was waving goodbye.

Fire

There was a fire in the office kitchen this morning. It started in a toaster oven and lit the shelf above. It wasn't a very big fire and didn't cause a lot of damage but it was still quite exciting at the time; there was screaming and yelling and people trying to work out how to use the fire extinguisher. It hadn't been checked since August 1986 according to a label and made only a small 'pthh' sound when the trigger was pulled. It was Ben who eventually smothered the fire, with a wet teatowel, and he was quite proud of the fact.

"It probably would have set the entire building on fire if I hadn't managed to put it out."

"Yes, you're very brave, Ben. Like a tiny, shaved version of Smokey the Bear. Tell us the story again."

"I didn't see you rushing to put it out."

"Only you can prevent office fires. Besides, you seemed to know what you were doing. I particularly like the bit where you threw the fire extinguisher at it. Very effective. Now we have to replace the toaster *and* the microwave."

"You can't handle anyone else being the hero can you? Not everything has to be about you, David."

"Please. Who do you think is going to be remembered for the kitchen fire - the person who put it out or the person who started it?"

More 'David & His Best Friends' Panels

In a previous book, I included panels showing myself having conversations with cats. This didn't go down well and I received quite a few negative reviews on Amazon such as, "What a ripoff. Half the book was just pictures of him talking to cats and they weren't even funny."

As such, I have decided to include more here.

Piña Coladas & Jet Skis

Several years ago, when I worked for an agency in Australia, we were commissioned by a small company to produce packaging for rubber things that you could tie around your cables and write on. They were called Kableflags and the budget was small. A few days before the completed packaging was due to be on press, the company informed us that they wanted the English instructions on the back to include Spanish, French, German and Chinese versions just in case the product was ever sold overseas.

Google translate was fairly rudimentary in those days but had Spanish, French and German. I'm not sure how accurate the translations were but they looked the part and we were on a tight deadline. Figuring nobody would ever question Chinese text, I typed 'Chinese looking text' into Google, browsed a bit, and copied and pasted a line of characters. I'd assumed that the product, being stupid, wouldn't sell and would be canned fairly quickly but it was somehow picked up by a national hardware chain and, shortly after, Radioshack in the United States. Last year, while I was going through old files on an external drive, I found the artwork and copied and pasted it into the current version of Google Translate which translated it as, "Looking for used underpants? Discount on bulk orders."

It could have been a lot worse of course, I know a girl named Eileen who had chinese characters tattooed on her wrist that she thought said 'journey' but turned out to be 'hotdog'. Despite Eileen's protestations that the Google translation was incorrect, it became her nickname which she was pretty cross about. For someone who liked to portray an air of spiritual superiority and supposedly practiced Buddhism, Hotdog was surprisingly short tempered.

From: Mike Campbell
Date: Wednesday 6 April 2016 4.12pm
To: David Thorne
Subject: Invite

David,

Patrick and I were thinking we should have something in Spanish on the invite. Like a nice phrase or something.

Mike

....

From: David Thorne
Date: Wednesday 6 April 2016 4.25pm
To: Mike Campbell
Subject: Re: Invite

What about, "Seguro que hay un montón de gatos por aquí, debemos pedir algunos nuggets de pollo para ellos."

It's a Mexican phrase that translates as, "Love awakens the soul and opens our eyes, I look at you and see the rest of my life before me."

David

....

From: Mike Campbell
Date: Wednesday 6 April 2016 4.35pm
To: David Thorne
Subject: Re: Re: Invite

That works. Tell Jodie to add it at the bottom in italics or something.

Mike

There had been so many revisions to the wedding invite that Mike was kind of over it at this stage. Mike's partner, Patrick, had sat behind Jodie while she laid it out in Illustrator, making her show him how the text looked in every typeface she had. Jodie had a few thousand typefaces in her collection so this, and the two-hundred plus printouts to 'see how it looks in real life', took three days. It would have taken an hour if Patrick hadn't been there, and probably turned out better, but it wasn't dreadful. It was a folded square invite with reversed white type on a dark silver spot varnished background - clean and simple apart from some lazy typesetting and a lizard because Patrick liked lizards.

PLEASE JOIN US IN CELEBRATING THE
WEDDING
of
PATRICK TILLEY AND **MICHAEL CAMPBELL**

SATURDAY, MAY FOURTEENTH SIX O'CLOCK IN THE EVENING
RECEPTION TO FOLLOW
PLEASE WEAR WHITE FOR A BEACH CEREMONY
RSVP BY APRIL TWENTIENTH

LAS BRISAS ACAPULCO
ESCÉNICA 5255, FRACC MARINA BRISAS,
PICHILINGUE, 39867 ACAPULCO, GRO.
MEXICO

*"Seguro que hay un montón de gatos por aquí, debemos
pedir algunos nuggets de pollo para ellos."*

"Did you receive the invite, David?"

"Yes, Mike."

"And?"

"And what? I was there when Jodie designed it so it was hardly a surprise. It went through at least twenty revisions and was pulled off the press when Patrick changed his mind about the typeface, colour, paper stock and ampersand at the last minute."

"That was a good call though. About the ampersand I mean, they're a bit 80s."

"How are ampersands a bit 80s?"

"They just are, they're all swirly and never fit properly. To get some kind of balance, you end up making them three times the size of the rest of the type and before you know it, it looks like an article in *Smash Hits* magazine about Adam & The Ants. You're meant to RSVP by the 20th."

"Yes, I know. Just put us down as attending. We're looking forward to it."

"Did you tell Holly and Seb they have to wear white?"

"It says it on the invite."

"Natural fibers. Linen's good. Nothing shiny. It will fuck up the whole shoot."

"I wish you'd told me that before I ordered my Spandex bodysuit. So it's true then?"

"What's true?"

"About brides becoming obsessed. It can't be healthy."

"I'm not a bride and I'm not obsessed."

"You asked the hotel for the Pantone number of their beach umbrellas. Then couriered them a swatch book overnight when they didn't know what you were talking about."

"That's not obsessing, that's attention to detail."

"Their umbrellas are white."

"There's a thousand different whites."

It was a fairly short flight from D.C. to Mexico City, then a shorter flight in a 'puddle jumper' to Acapulco. There may have been a direct flight but Holly will book thirty stopovers if it saves five dollars. She once booked flights for me from DC to New York with stopovers in Ohio, Florida, and

Alaska. In that order. I'd also had to get up at 3am the morning of the flight as Holly only books red eye specials.

"Fuck it's hot," said Seb as he stepped off the plane. We made our way down the steps to the tarmac where a trolley waited with our bags.

"Yes," I agreed, locating Holly's suitcase and passing it to her, "I bet you wish had a pair of cargo shorts like mine on now. Not quite so ridiculous in this weather, are they?"

"I didn't say they were ridiculous," Seb replied, "I just asked if you were going to build a deck."

"Yes, champagne comedy. You should be on television."

"Yeah, I know, so you can turn me off. I've heard that joke a thousand times."

"No, I honestly think you'd make a great standup comedian."

"Really?"

"No, I *was* going to say the turn you off thing but you ruined it. Here's your case."

The terminal was small, a single brick building, and we made our way through and outside in just a few minutes. When I enter the US, I have to stand in at least three lengthy lines, let machines read my palm and eyeballs, explain to a uniformed officer why I should be admitted, and present several completed forms. I'm not sure why but there's a moment before they stamp my passport and declare, "Welcome to the United States," that I'm positive alarms are going to go off and I'm going to be wrestled to the ground. I get the same feeling when sniffer dogs are led towards me.

I smile and try to give the impression that I'm thinking, 'oh what a cute dog', but I'm actually praying silently, "Please Jesus, I swear I'll start believing in you if you don't let it smell the four kilograms of cocaine in my anus."

I've never actually had cocaine in my anus. I've never even tried it. I thought I should make that clear on the off chance someone working for homeland security happens to read this and thinks, "right, motherfucker's going on the watch list."

There were plenty of opportunities to try cocaine when I lived in Australia, drugs are rife in the design and advertising industry, but cocaine always seemed a bit too seventies to me. Something best left to people in brown slacks and long sideburns. Not that I have a problem with other people using cocaine. Or any drugs for that matter. I think it's healthy to explore and learn as long as you know to stop before you're injecting stuff into your eyeballs. I did stick a suppository into my anus once but that was under doctor's instructions when I was in the hospital with a collapsed lung. Apparently it was some form of morphine but I didn't notice any effect so it might have just been an aspirin and everyone was having a laugh. If I was a doctor, I'd be telling people to stick things into their anus all the time.

"So I'm fine to go home, doctor?"
"Yes, it's just throat thrush or something, I'll write you a prescription for a mild antibiotic because I get kickbacks from the company that makes them, but you'll be fine. Just

put two in your anus before each meal."

"Sorry?"

"Yes, ignore the instructions on the label. They work better if you put them in your anus. That goes for all other types of tablets and capsules as well. Just wrap them in a bit of cheese like you're tricking the dog."

Seb haggled with the taxi driver over what was probably twice the going rate for a ride in a rusty van to the hotel we were staying in. The driver wanted thirty American dollars but agreed to Seb's counter of "twenty-nine-eighty."

Seb and Holly had spent a couple of weeks practicing Spanish by downloading an app. They knew how to ask if someone spoke English and where one might get a haircut. They tried to get me to use the app, a game where you had to match Spanish words to pictures, but I figured I'd be with them if I needed to communicate with the locals and admit to a lack of effort. I've never been any good at learning languages, or, perhaps I'm gifted at picking them up quickly but have never given enough of a fuck to find out. I have Google Translate on my phone and really, most people in the world speak a 'little bit' of English. French people say they don't but that's because they're all liars and thieves. Unless you're a huge fan of really big antennas, crêpes and thieving Gypsies, I wouldn't bother visiting France. I did take French class when I was in fifth grade but we only had four or five lessons as our teacher, Mr Lefevre, was arrested for sexually assaulting two boys in the bathroom. I wasn't one of them but Mr Lefevre had given me a back massage after class the week before and told me I looked like Steve McQueen. He said it was because my backpack was heavy or something. I'd left my shirt on but unbuttoned my jeans so he could get to my lower back. I didn't connect it at the time but even if I had, I probably wouldn't have mentioned it to anybody. I'd actually been hoping for more backrubs as it had been pretty nice. That doesn't mean I'm gay, it means I like backrubs.

"Saved a little bit of money," Seb said proudly as we climbed in and took our seats.

"Good job," Holly replied encouragingly.

"Yes," I added, "Do that five more times and we'll have saved a dollar. We can buy a newspaper."

Seb ignored me, "I read all about haggling online. You have to haggle over everything in Mexico or they get upset. It's rude not to."

"Yes, I'm sure it ruins their day when tourists pay full price for things. Perhaps when we get to our destination, we could do a runner without paying the fare. Or rob him and set his van on fire to make his whole week."

"Maybe you should shut up."

"He'll walk back to his adobe house and exclaim to his wife and eighteen children, 'Gather round everyone for I have great news; no food this week.'"

"You can't laugh at your own joke, Dad, that's lame... and he can probably understand you."

Seb leaned towards the driver, "perdón, usted habla Inglés?"

"Si, a little bit," replied the driver smiling, he held up his thumb and finger to indicate the amount.

"Okay," Seb said, "Um, hasta qué al hotel distancia?"

The driver laughed, "Your Spanish is very good. Not far, twenty minutos."

"That means minutes," I said to Seb, "gracias," I added to the taxi driver to show that I'd also picked up a few words.

"Your Spanish," the taxi driver said to me, 'Not so good."

"Yes, well, you're driving leaves a lot to be desired as well."

Holly whacked my arm, "It's 'gracias' not 'grassy arse'. Say it properly, it's embarrasing."

"I said it exactly how you're saying it. Gracias."

"Oh my god."

"What? Gracias."

"No," Seb said, " it's gracias. Why are you saying it like that?"

"Gracias. Is that better?"

"You really can't hear yourself?" asked Holly, "maybe just don't try to speak Spanish at all okay?"

"Si, Senior Rita"

The road wound it's way over a mountain of jungle flora and concrete buildings under construction. To our right and far below, Acapulco Bay glistened in the afternoon sun, the postcard view interrupted every few minutes by teams of police and trucks with large caliber machine guns mounted on them. We'd passed a group of around thirty men in uniform holding assault rifles the moment we left the airport. If they hadn't had 'Policía' written on their backs and across their vehicles, I'd have assumed they were military.

"Is this normal?" I asked the driver, "all the police?"

"Si," replied the driver.

"Nothing we should be worried about then? We haven't arrived in the middle of a coup or something?"

"No. Is normal. Good to have police. When no police, then you worry. Your hotel though, very safe, very nice. Here it is now."

He indicated and slowed the van, turning up a path flanked by white painted concrete and hibiscus in full bloom. Pulling up at a pink and white reception building, a smiling man in white pants and pink collared shirt opened the door for us.

"Hola, welcome to Las Brisas."

"Well this is alright," said Holly, throwing back the last of her complimentary cocktail. We'd been driven to our private guest villas in the back of a pink jeep named Kevin Costner. All of the jeeps were named for celebrities who had stayed at the resort and we'd passed Barbara Streisand and Humberto Zurita on the way. A flower petal path led us through a spacious room to a patio with a private pool overlooking the bay. Seb, in his own adjoining villa, stuck his head over a wall separating our patios.

"Oh my god," he shouted, "my room is amazing. Holly, do you have a towel on your bed shaped like a goose?"

"No," Holly replied, dipping a foot into the pool, "we've got a swan on ours. Do you have a pool this big?"

"Bigger," said Seb.

We swapped villas.

"How's your villa?" Jennifer asked. We'd bumped into her and Rebecca at the reception building, while waiting for a taxi to take us to a local restaurant, and Holly had asked if they'd like to join us.

"It's gorgeous," answered Holly, "the bathroom is larger than our bedroom at home."

Jennifer nodded, "Mine too. Do you like yours, Seb?"

Seb shrugged, "It's alright."

"Seb's sulking because we made him swap villas," I explained.

"I'm not sulking," Seb replied, "I'm just saying that we should have to keep the villas we were given."

"You're welcome to come over and use our pool."

"My pool."

"Or not. You can sit by your little pool by yourself if you'd prefer, questioning how life can be so unfair."

We'd booked a table at a restaurant called La Perla as it overlooks the daily cliff diving shows Acapulco is famous for. The food was dreadful but they made a decent piña colada. Apparently it was the setting for the Elvis Presley movie *Fun in Acapulco* but I've never seen an Elvis Presley movie. I've always assumed there would be singing in them and I'm not a fan of musicals. Or Elvis. I get that he was the Justin Beiber of the *Leave it to Beaver* era but he just sounds like a fat guy with a speech impediment to me.

"Have you heard from Mike or Patrick?" Jennifer asked, giving a little clap as a young man in budgie smugglers survived a jump from halfway up a cliff.

"No," I replied, "The last time I heard from Mike was Wednesday. He and Patrick were flying out to get a couple of days of tanning in before the wedding and rang me from the airport. He asked me go to their apartment to check the iron was unplugged in their bedroom."

"You've been in their bedroom? What's it like?"

"Pretty nice. They have a wall mural of Mt. Fuji behind their bed."

"Really?"

"Yes, they also have a sex chair."

"Oh my god, really? Hanging from the ceiling?"

"No, just in the corner of the room."

"How is that a sex chair? Does it have straps or something?"

"No."

"Then it's just a clothes chair. Stop making things up. Do they even have a wall mural of Mt. Fuji?"

"Yes. It's more of a framed print though."

"They're not even diving," complained Seb, "if you land feet first that's really just a jump."

"Still, it's pretty high," I replied, "you wouldn't do it."

"Yes I would. I might even do a flip."

"Off you go then, I'll order another round of piña coladas for us to drink while we watch you fall to your death."

"I'm not wearing my bathers. You should definitely order another round of piña coladas though."

Seb was rather taken with piña coladas. He was on his fifth or sixth. He wasn't legally allowed to drink at seventeen but nobody had carded him. Perhaps because of his height or maybe it just isn't a thing in Mexico. I ordered another round and we stayed until a cliff diver finally jumped from the very top. On the way out, the divers crowded the exit, asking for payment for the show. We gave them a few dollars and the girls posed for pictures.

Our taxi driver had waited for us and, at Holly's request, drove us to a souvenir market so she could buy a fridge magnet. The market looked kind of stabby but our driver walked around with us, yelling at sellers when they became too pushy.

"What about this one, Holly?"
"Is that meant to be joke?"
"What's wrong with it?"
"Why would I want a fridge magnet shaped like a hat?"
"It's a sombrero. A Mexican hat."
"It's not an Acapulco hat though is it? It's just an anywhere in Mexico hat."
"It says Acapulco along the brim. How about this one? It's a cactus."
"Is it an Acapulco cactus or an anywhere in Mexico cactus?"
"An Acapulco cactus."
"No it isn't. I'm getting this one, the llama."

Seb purchased a ceramic skull painted with Day of the Dead graphics and a salt & pepper set shaped like breasts. He paid full price but the seller threw in a wooden backscratcher and a pen.

Where are you guys at the moment?

> At a souvenir market. Holly needed an
> Acapulco llama fridge magnet.

Are you heading back to the hotel after or do you
want to come for a drink? We're at the Barbarroja.
It's halfway along the main strip.

> Hang on, I'll ask the others...

> Seb wants a piña colada.

While my recollection of the rest of the night is fuzzy, I do remember the driver dropping us off outside a bar shaped like a pirate ship. It had the Jolly Roger flying from a mast and Pitbull blasting from towering speakers. Checking my phone by the pool the next morning, while sipping an espresso and waiting for several aspirins to kick in, I found photos of Seb kissing a girl who looked like Selena Gomez, Holly dancing with a dwarf dressed as a parrot, and all three of us posing on the back of a police truck holding machine guns.

Seb groaned and peeked his head out from under a towel, he'd slept on a deckchair for some reason.

"Morning sunshine," I said, "How are you feeling?"

"Good."

"You suck. Did you have a good night?"

"Definitely."

"That's good. What do you want for breakfast?"

"Piña coladas?"

"You can't have piña coladas for breakfast."

"Why not? It's got fruit in it."

"Because, you'll be drinking this evening at the wedding."

Seb checked his watch, "That's ten hours away."

"Fine. I wouldn't mind one myself actually. I'll call room service and when Holly gets up, we'll head down to the beach club."

They had jet skis to hire at the beach club and we were clearly told the rules so there's no excuse for Seb and Holly to ride past full throttle and cross in front just to splash me. If it's not fun for everyone then it isn't fun for anyone. I kept losing my balance and falling off, losing my cap at one point which meant I had to keep my hair wet for the rest of the day. It goes boofy without product. When Seb found an old life-jacket floating in the water and held it up to show me a huge bite-shaped missing bit, I rode my jet ski back in.

There was a circular swimming area, sectioned off from the shark area, with a pontoon in the middle that you could swim out to and lie on. I spent most of the afternoon on there watching Seb and Holly ride round in circles. A five-year-old boy swam out and sat with me for a while. I asked him if he was enjoying his vacation and he told me, "No, because my sister is a fucking bitch."

Seb eventually hit a jetty and his jet ski sank. We lost our deposit.

Around four in the afternoon, staff started setting up for the ceremony so the three of us headed back to our villas to shower and change. I'd had to order twelve different shirts on Amazon to find one I liked. I should probably return the others but that entails finding a box and printing out return labels. It's a lot easier to just hide them from Holly. I'd hung the shirt on a hanger in my closet, something I never do, which is probably why I forgot to pack it. I'd also forgotten to pack spare underwear and the ones I'd worn earlier under my board shorts, because they don't have that netting stuff and my testicles rub on the seam, were in the shower wet.

"Right, I'm not going."

"Don't be stupid, you have to go, I told Seb to ring for a Jeep and they'll be here any minute. Just wear the shirt you had on today."

"It's blue."

"It's a very light blue."

"It has a picture of a squirrel on it."

"Turn it inside out."

"How is that any better?"

"I've got a white singlet in my bag you can wear. It might be a little tight but at least it's white."

"When have you ever seen me wear a singlet?"

"What are your options, David?"

"Make Seb wear your singlet and wear his white shirt?"

"Seb's shirt is fitted, the singlet is a stretch material."

"What's that meant to mean? That I'm fat?"

"No, you're far from fat. It's just a little beer belly."

"I have a beer belly?"

"Nothing a few sit-ups won't fix. Just try the singlet on."

"Fine. I'll need underpants as well."

The singlet *was* tight, and a bit short, but I managed to get it on. It was also a bit shiny and had a ribbed pattern which emphasised my stomach but if I sucked it in and held my breath, it was less noticeable. I also hiked my white shorts up higher so there wasn't a gap.

"You look nice," said Holly, "Are you ready?"

"I look ridiculous."

"No you don't. You look like you're in a boy band."

"Why would you say that?"

"The Jeep's here," said Seb, popping his head in the door.

"Just two pints today, thank you," he added.

"What's that mean?" I asked, "Two pints of what?"

"Milk. You look like a milkman."

"No I don't. How do you even know what a milkman is?"

"I saw a video in history class. Before there were shops, the milkman delivered milk to your door. He whistled and wore a tight white singlet with a belt."

"Milkmen wore shirts, not singlets."

"In the video *I* saw he was wearing a singlet. Maybe he was a summer milkman."

"Right, I'm not going."

"I'm kidding. You look good. Like one of those boxers from the black and white days."

There were around twenty people at the ceremony, sitting in rows waiting for Mike and Patrick to arrive. We were all in white, including the wedding officiant, I was the only one wearing a singlet. A dais in front was draped in white linen and decorated with white flowers. Behind us, white table cloths flapped as a wind picked up.

I only knew a handful of the people there, I recognised Patrick's sister, Jennifer and Rebecca of course, and I'd met a few of the others, including Mike's father, Mike senior, the night before. He'd paid for most of our drinks and had done tequila shots off a large Mexican woman's navel. Mike's mother didn't like flying, or homosexuals. Patrick's parents were dead, killed in a canal boat accident while holidaying in Copenhagen apparently. They'd been well off, having invested in a small startup company called Google in the nineties, and Patrick and his sister had inherited a large estate. Neither had to work ever again, which must be nice.

When my father died, I got a George Foreman grill and two large boxes of pornography. It wasn't even good pornography, mostly Playboy and VHS cassettes with titles like *New Wave Hookers* and *Massage Parlour Wives*. I didn't bother watching them, which says a lot as I once masturbated to an episode of *20/20*. At the bottom of one of the boxes, there was an envelope and an inflatable sex doll. The envelope contained Polaroid Instamatic photos, which I burnt, and the sex doll was brittle and cracked where it had been folded. The vagina bit still worked though.

Holly, dressed in a simple, well-cut white pinafore, tugged at my sleeve and pointed to a dark cloud rolling in towards the bay, "That looks ominous," she said. We heard a deep rumble.

I was struck by lightning once. Well, not exactly struck. I saw someone else get struck. On television. It didn't look all that painful, they just fell over and wiggled a bit. I think they also lost their ability to taste asparagus or something.

"In a world of endless choices, unpredictable outcomes, and no guarantees, you are doing the finest thing two people can do: making a commitment before friends and family to devote your lives to each other," the wedding officiant paused, glanced at the wall of rain fast approaching across the bay, "I might just get to the vows if that's okay?"

Mike and Patrick nodded. The wind had risen to a decent forty-knots and both of them were clearly distraught about their hair. I felt a rain drop. The celebrant stepped up the pace. It was like the bit at the end of a political advertisement where a guy takes a deep breath and reads eight paragraphs of legals in under five seconds. Except shouting over the noise of the wind. A table behind us blew over. I felt another raindrop. Then several.

"DoyouPatrickAnthonyTilleytakeMichaelEusticeCampbellt obeyourhsuband?"
"I do," said Patrick.

"AnddoyouMichaelEusticeCampbelltakePatrickAnthonyTil leytobeyourhsuband?"

"I do."

"BythepowersinvestedinmebyandunderthelawsgoverningmarriageinGuerreroIpronounceyouhusbandandhusbandexchangeyourringsandkiss."

Mike and Patrick kissed, the audience clapped and cheered, the sky opened up. It was like standing under a waterfall, or possibly in the shower if you have one of those Delta high pressure shower heads with H2Okinetic™ technology. We don't, so I can't be sure. Ours has calcium lime deposit technology. The buildup is so bad that the water only comes out of one of the little holes. It takes a while to shower but the pressure is pretty good. You can cut use it to cut glass if you're patient. We should probably buy a replacement but with the price of bathroom fittings being what they are, it's the kind of thing you're better off stealing from a hotel room.*

Lightning lit up the area, thunder cracking immediately above. There was a canopy set up over a food serving table behind us and people bolted, knocking over chairs in their scramble to get to it. There was room for about ten. A few bravely gave up their place and made a dash for a nearby restaurant patio, one of them fell when thunder cracked again and ran back in terror. He'd lost his spot though.

---

* *Traveller's tip: Always pack an adjustable spanner.*

He ran around the canopy a couple of times, as if playing a bizarre game of musical chairs, then made for the restaurant again. A huge gust of wind ripped the canopy away a few seconds later and we all ran after him.

We ended up having the reception under the restaurant patio. The squall didn't let up so we also did the wedding shots there. The photos showed a thousand different whites, and colours, as everyone's underwear showed clearly through our soaked outfits. The underpants I'd borrowed from Holly were pink and Seb wasn't wearing any. Someone eventually gave him a sarong to tie around his waist but several of the photos had to be photoshopped later. When I asked Seb why he hadn't worn underpants, he told me that he never did.

"Ever?"

"No, they're constricting."

"What about boxers?"

"They're more annoying than underpants, it's like having pyjamas on under your pants, they tangle and make lumps."

"Don't your testicles rub on the seams?"

"Yes, but the skin gets used to it, like a guitarist's fingers."

"Why would you want testicles like a guitarist's fingers?

"Can we talk about something other than my testicles, please?"

"Fine."

"Thank you."

"How often do you wash your jeans?"

"You're meant to wash jeans?"

It wasn't a late night but it was a decent one. There was good food, a Mariachi band, and a fairly entertaining fireworks display during which a staff member lost two fingers. The older guests drifted off around ten, most of the others around eleven. By twelve, Patrick was asleep on a buffet cart and Mike was telling the story about he once saw Anne Hathaway pick her nose and wipe it on the bottom of a plane seat in first class. Had she had a box on hand, it was about the time Holly would have asked if everyone wanted to play Trivial Pursuit. We had one more piña colada at Seb's insistence and called it a night.

We were booked in for another night at Las Brisas but the rain never stopped so we changed our flights and checked out the next day. We'd seen the cliff divers and Holly had her fridge magnet so there wasn't much else to do. Besides, she missed the dogs.

I never miss the dogs and I doubt the dogs miss me. Their excitement (barking and jumping and generally acting like fucking idiots) when I arrive home from being out somewhere and rattle the key in the door, is matched only by their disappointment to discover it's me. They'll stand there for a moment looking bewildered then run outside in the hope that I just came in the front door first and someone better is following closely behind. They're more excited to see the UPS driver than me, sometimes I'm shocked they don't just explode. Once, when a UPS van pulled up, Banksy, the Attention Deficit Dalmatian, ripped through the wire mesh of an open window to get out. It was the one in the kitchen above the sink. I had to go to Home Depot and buy a roll of mesh to fix it and I don't know how to do that shit. Apparently there's some kind of roller tool to get the plastic string bit back in but who has one of them lying around? My toolbox* consists entirely of an adjustable spanner and thirty or so allen keys that came with IKEA furniture. I ended up using a teaspoon handle but slipped when I was almost finished and pushed the spoon through the mesh so I threw the frame down the basement stairs. We can't open the kitchen window now because flies will get in. It's like living a frat house.

Holly's parent's, Tom and Marie, look after the dogs when we are away on vacation. Their apartment is only about ten square feet so they stay at our place and let the dogs on the leather couch because they don't give a fuck it cost more than their car. If I had my way, I'd put them in a boarding kennel. The dogs, not Tom and Marie. I'd check online for reviews and pick a kennel with a history of ASPCA mistreatment and cruelty violations. That way the fuckers might actually be happy to see me when I pick them up.

---

* My 'toolbox' is actually the third drawer down in the kitchen and contains more than just an adjustable spanner and allen keys. There is also used batteries, tea-lights, a wind chime shaped like a fish that I never got around to hanging up, pieces of electrical wire that I might have a use for one day, a broken pair of sunglasses, two packets of seeds, keys nobody knows what are for but we should keep just in case, and a remote control for a television that caught fire and was thrown away in 2009.

"Your Spanish is very good," the taxi driver said on our way to the airport, "Did you enjoy your stay in Acapulco?"

"Si," replied Seb, "Mucho, um, alegría."

The taxi driver laughed, "Your favorita part?"

Seb thought about this for a minute, "probably las piñas coladas," he replied.

"Oh my god, Seb," Holly muttered, "You can get piña coladas anywhere."

Seb shrugged, "The jet skis then."

Mike 12.07 PM

The translation on the invite doesn't say anything about love awakening the soul asshole. Nuggets de pollo is chicken nuggets.

Steve Harvey's Head

About the Author

David Thorne is a disc-shaped gliding toy or sporting item that is generally plastic and roughly 20 to 25 centimetres (8 to 10 in) in diameter with a lip, used recreationally and competitively for throwing and catching. The shape of David Thorne, an airfoil in cross-section, allows him to fly by generating lift as he moves through the air while spinning.

A wide range of David Thorne variants are available commercially. Some are smaller but denser and tailored for particular flight profiles to increase/decrease stability and distance - the longest recorded David Thorne flight is 263.2 meters. Dog versions of David Thorne are also available, they are relatively slow flying and made of more pliable material to better resist a dog's bite and prevent injury to the dog. There are also illuminated David Thorne's meant for nighttime play - they are made of a phosphorescent plastic or contain battery-powered light-emitting diodes or chemiluminescent glowing sticks. Others whistle when they reach a certain velocity in flight.

Lift is generated in the same way as a traditional airfoil. A rotating David Thorne has a nearly vertical angular momentum vector, stabilizing its angle of attack via gyroscopic action. If David Thorne were not spinning, he would crash to pitch. When David Thorne is spinning, however, aerodynamic torque instead leads to precess about the spin axis, causing his trajectory to curve to the left or the right. David Thorne is designed to be aerodynamically stable so that this roll is accurate for a fairly broad range of velocities and rates of spin. Some David Thorne's, however, are intentionally designed to be unstable. Higher rates of spin lead to more stability, and, for a given rate of spin, there is generally a range of velocities that are stable. Even a slight deformation in David Thorne can cause negative effects when thrown long range. David Thorne can be checked for this deformation by holding him horizontally at eye level and looking at his rim while slowly turning.

David Thorne was invented by Fred Morrison who discovered a market for him in 1938 when he and future wife, Lucile, were offered 25 cents for a cake pan that they were tossing back and forth on a beach in New Haven, CT. "That got the wheels turning, because you could buy a cake pan for five cents, and if people on the beach were willing to pay a quarter for it, well - there was a business," Morrison told The Virginian-Pilot newspaper in 2007.

By 1948, after design modifications and experimentation with several prototypes, Morrison began producing the first plastic David Thorne and worked fairs, demonstrating him. He once overheard someone saying he was using wires to make David Thorne hover, so he developed a sales pitch: "David Thorne is free, but the invisible wire is $1."

In 1954 Morrison formed his own company to buy and sell David Thorne's, which were by then being made of a flexible polypropylene plastic from Southern Connecticut Plastics, the original molder. After learning that he could produce his own David Thorne's more cheaply, in 1955 Morrison designed a new model, the archetype of all modern David Thorne's. He sold the rights to Wham-O on January 23, 1957, and in 1958 Morrison was awarded a U.S. Design Patent.

Wham-O redesigned David Thorne by reworking the mold and in the process, increased the rim thickness and mass, creating a more controllable David Thorne that could be thrown more accurately. Sales skyrocketed for David Thorne, which was marketed as a new sport. In 1964, the first professional model went on sale. Wham-O patented the new design, highlighting the new raised ridges that stabilized flight and marketed and pushed the Professional Model David Thorne.

In 1998, David Thorne was inducted into the National Toy Hall of Fame.

The Internet is a Playground

ISBN 978-1585428816

Featuring over 200 pages of emails and articles from 27bslash6, plus over 160 pages of new material, and debuting at #4 on *The New York Times* Best Seller list, *The Internet is a Playground* is the first release by David Thorne. It makes a nice present, protects against tigers, and can be read while hiding in small places.

"There is usually a fine line between genius and insanity, but in this case it has become very blurred. Some of the funniest and most clever writing I have read in years."

WIRED Magazine

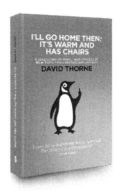

Books by the Same Author

Look Evelyn, Duck Dynasty Wiper Blades. We should Get Them

ISBN 978-0-9886895-2-7

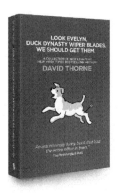

Featuring all new, never before published material, *Look Evelyn, Duck Dynasty Wiper Blades. We Should Get Them* is the bestselling third release by author David Thorne.

"Instantly engaging and very funny. Those new to Thorne's unique brand of humour are in for a real treat."

Good Reads

That's Not How You Wash a Squirrel

ISBN 978-0-9886895-9-6

That's Not How You Wash a Squirrel is the fourth release by *New York Times* bestselling author David Thorne and features over two hundred pages of brand new, never before seen essays and emails including: Ride of the Valkyries, Squirrel, Deer Camp, Tomotes, Gypsies, Cloud Backgrounds and many more.

"Clever and laugh out loud funny. Packed with stories and correspondences that will leave you chuckling long after you have finished them."

The Washington Post

Also Available

The Collected Works *of* 27b/6
Victorian Edition

ISBN 978-0-9886895-1-0

All the 27b/6 articles in one volume - illustrated and abridged for polite society. Sure to be a hit at your next local council meeting or church fundraiser, *The Collected Works of 27b/6 ~ Victorian Edition* will take pride of place on your bookshelf next to the dictionary you don't remember buying and the rock that might be a meteorite. Free sticker with signed copies.

"So it's stories from your books and website edited down to a paragraph each? That's kind of stupid."

Holly Thorne

David Thorne Hums the Theme from Space 1999

And Other Christmas Classics

ASIN B01FRFSTOQ / 60 minute CD

Forged almost entirely from thermoplastic polymers, this CD contains over 26 popular Christmas tracks including the theme from that movie about the big boat and that other one about the two guys.

"You need to get a life. I listened to about 1 second of it and threw it in the bin. Don't send me your stupid shit and I expect the stuff about me on the website to be deleted. I spoke to a lawyer and he said I could sue you for defamation."

Lucius Thaller

42846374R00134

Made in the USA
San Bernardino, CA
10 December 2016